DO YOU KNOW

# Chameleons?

Written by
**Alain M. Bergeron
Michel Quintin
Sampar**

Illustrations by
**Sampar**

Translated by
**Solange Messier**

Fitzhenry & Whiteside

First published as "Savais-tu? Les Caméléons" by Éditions Michel Quintin, Québec, Canada

Published in Canada by Fitzhenry & Whiteside, 195 Allstate Parkway, Markham, Ontario L3R 4T8
Published in the United States by Fitzhenry & Whiteside, 311 Washington Street, Brighton, Massachusetts 02135



www.fitzhenry.ca godwit@fitzhenry.ca

10 9 8 7 6 5 4 3 2 1

Library and Archives Canada Cataloguing in Publication
Do You Know Chameleons?
ISBN 9781554552993 (pbk.)
Data available on file

Publisher Cataloging-in-Publication Data (U.S.)
Do You Know Chameleons?
ISBN 9781554552993 (pbk.)
Data available on file

Fitzhenry & Whiteside acknowledges with thanks the Canada Council for the Arts, and the Ontario Arts Council for their support of our publishing program. We acknowledge the financial support of the Government of Canada through the Canada Book Fund (CBF) for our publishing activities.

Canada Council for the Arts
Conseil des Arts du Canada

ONTARIO ARTS COUNCIL
CONSEIL DES ARTS DE L'ONTARIO
50 YEARS OF ONTARIO GOVERNMENT SUPPORT OF THE ARTS
50 ANS DE SOUTIEN DU GOUVERNEMENT DE L'ONTARIO AUX ARTS

Text and cover design by Daniel Choi
Cover image by Sampar
Printed in Canada by Friesens.

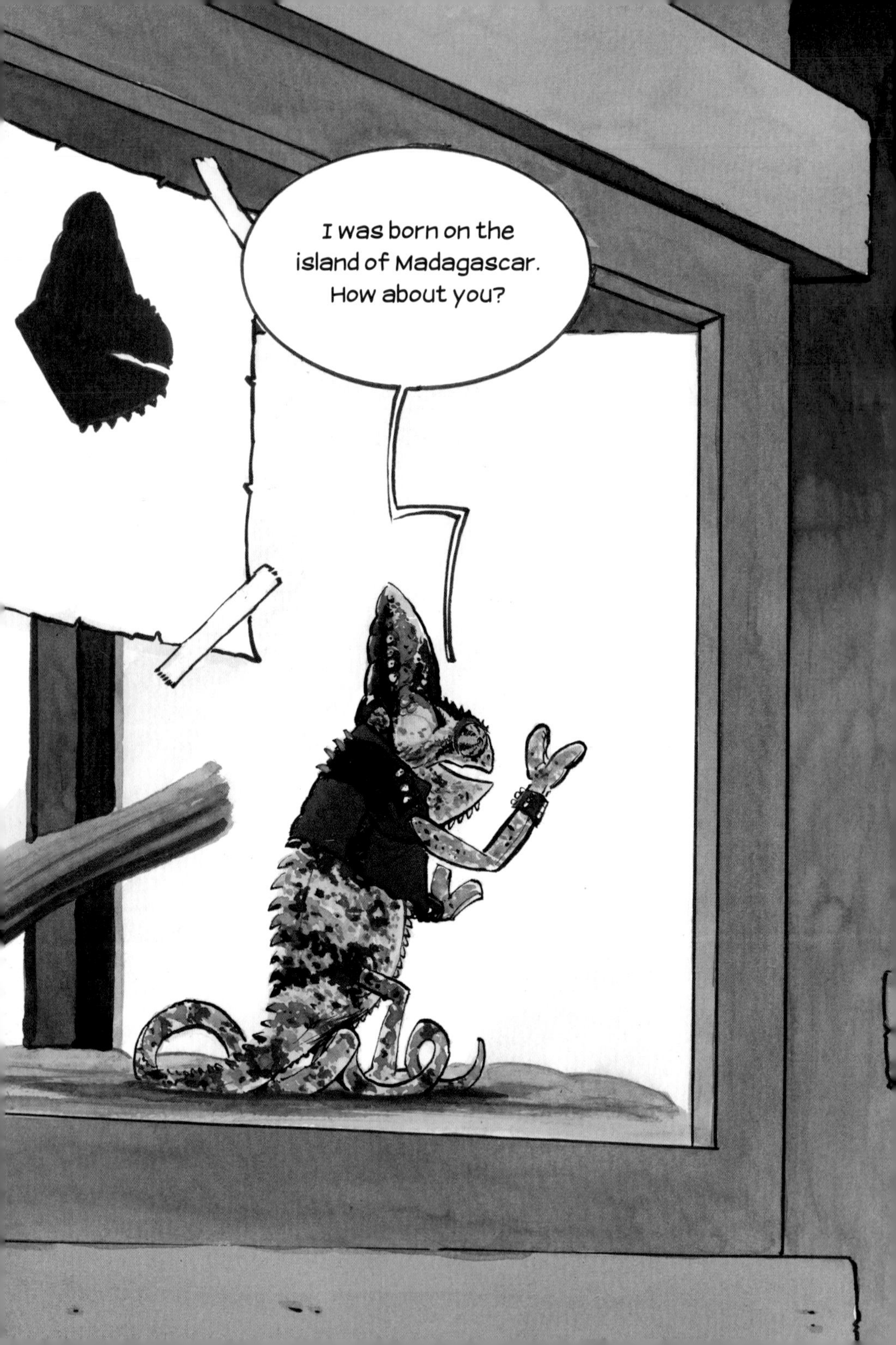
I was born on the island of Madagascar. How about you?

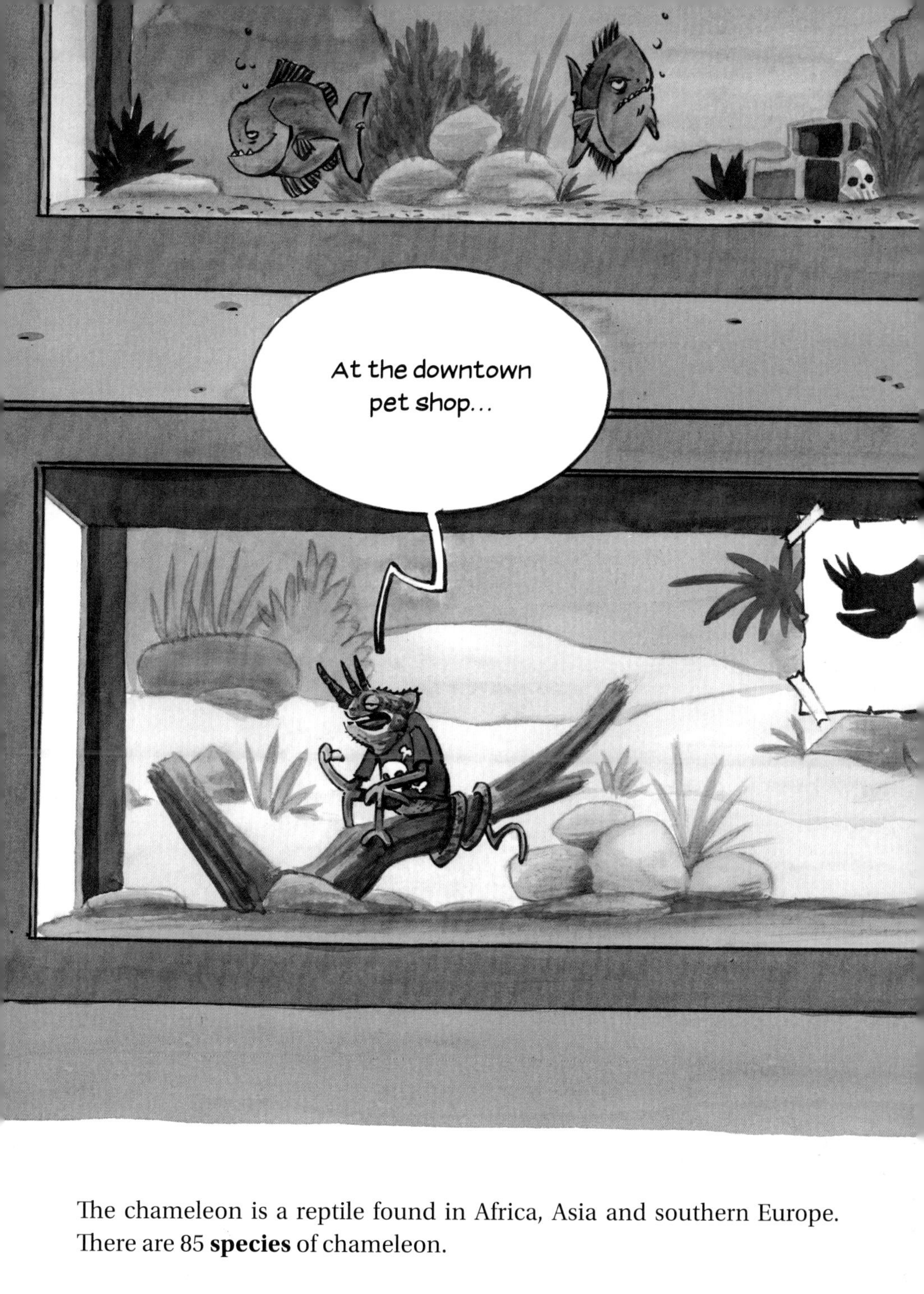
At the downtown pet shop...

The chameleon is a reptile found in Africa, Asia and southern Europe. There are 85 **species** of chameleon.

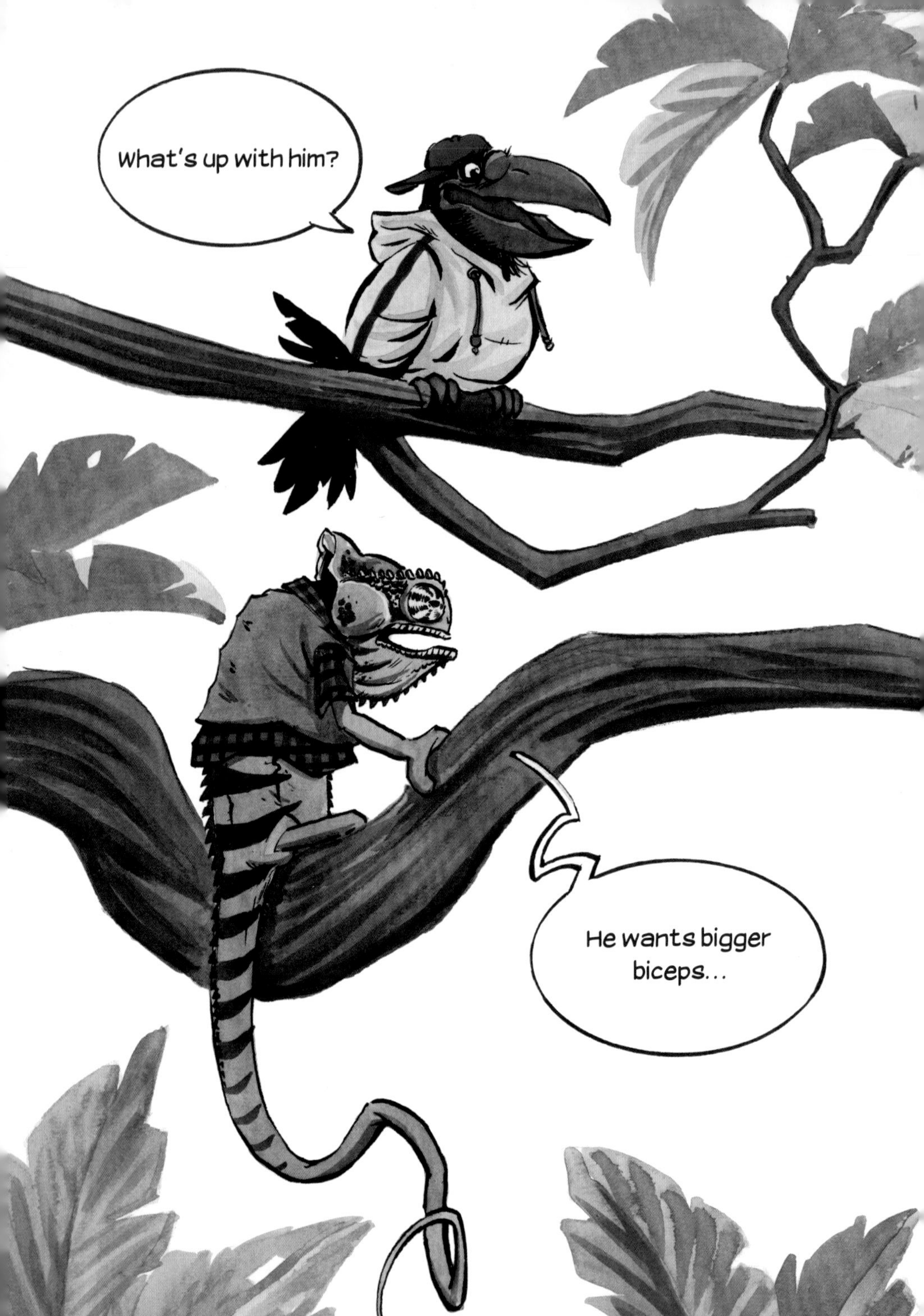
What's up with him?
He wants bigger biceps...

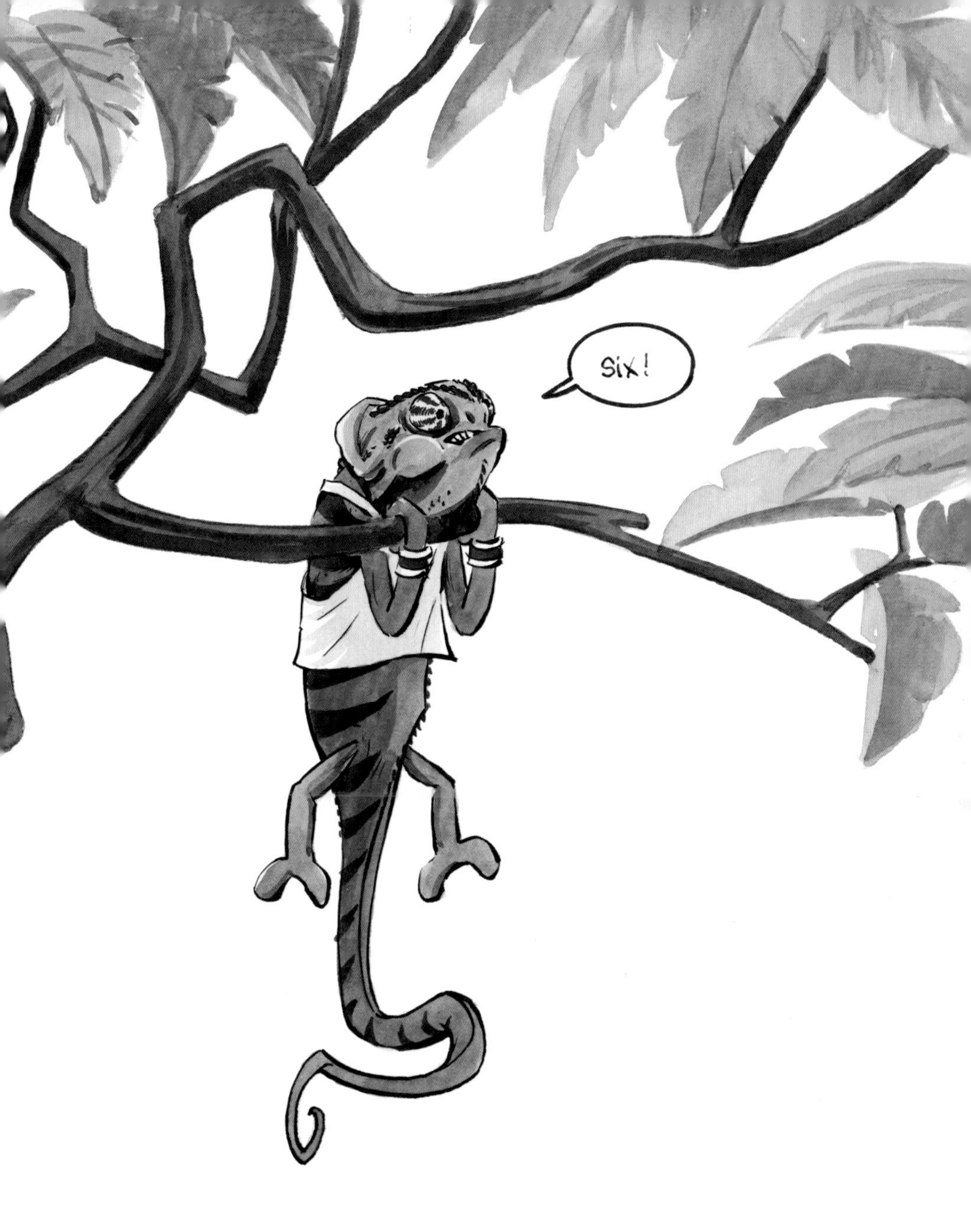
SIX!

Apart from a few species that live in desert regions, chameleons are **arboreal**. Their pincer-like fingers help them climb trees.

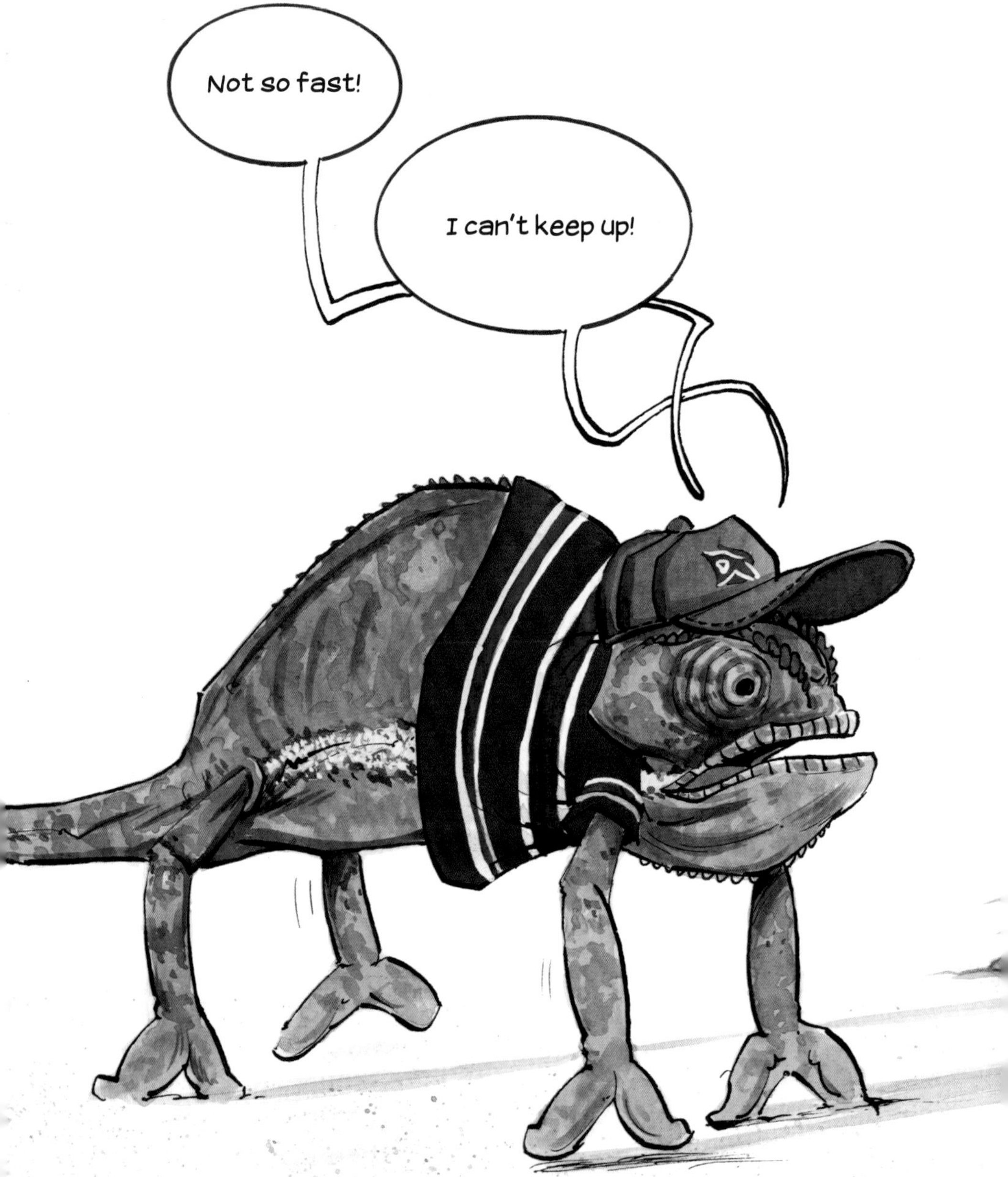
Not so fast!
I can't keep up!

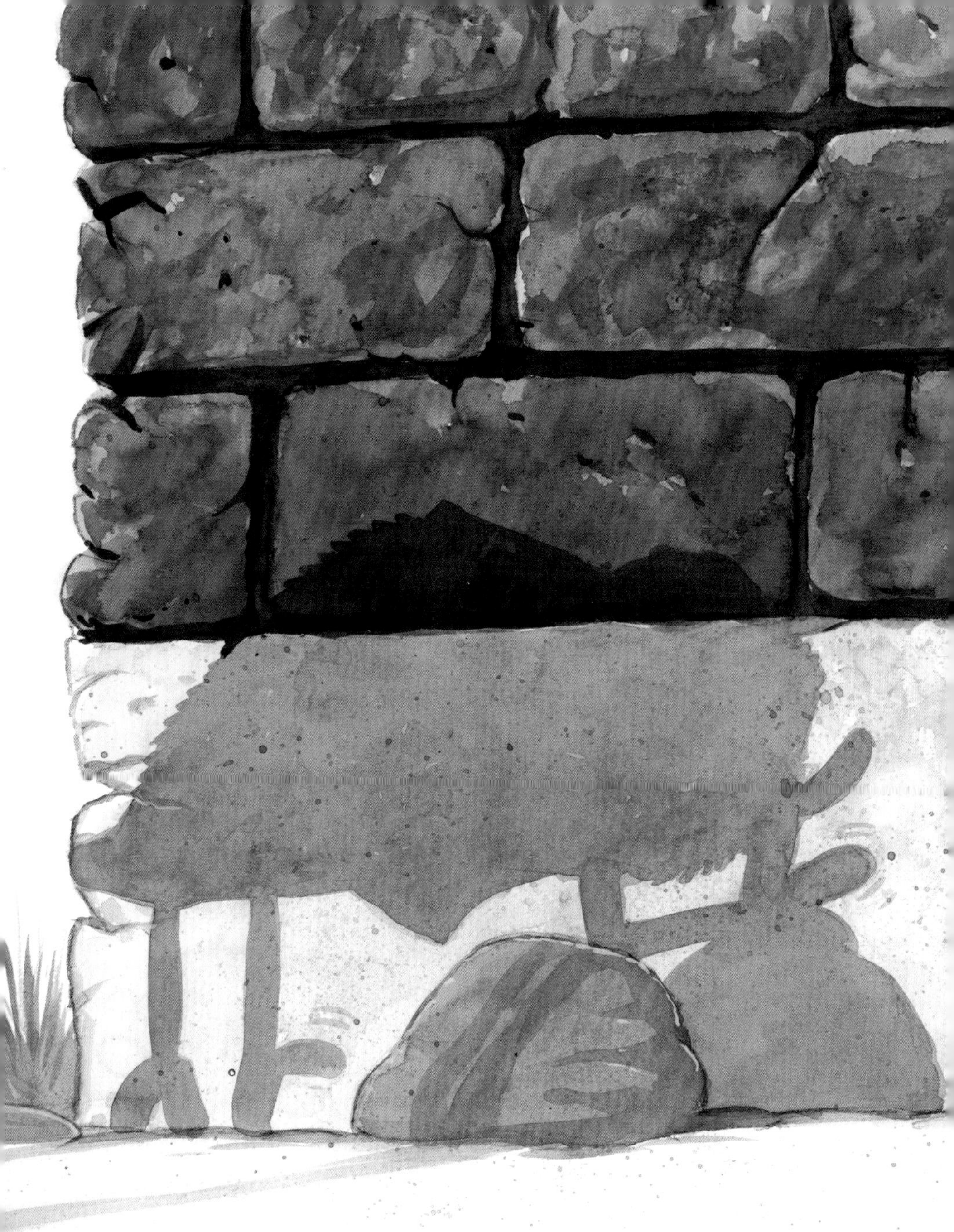

These lizards move extremely slowly and are most active during the day.

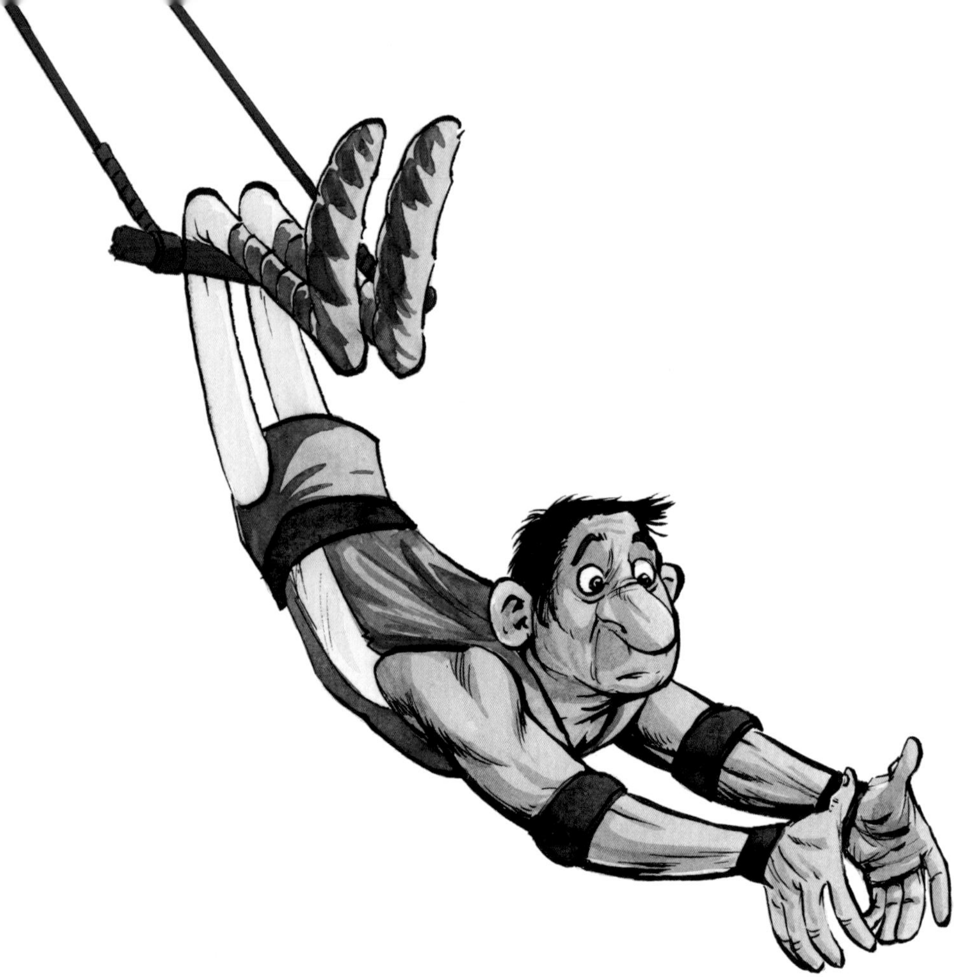

Most species possess **prehensile tails**, which they wrap around vegetation to facilitate their movements.

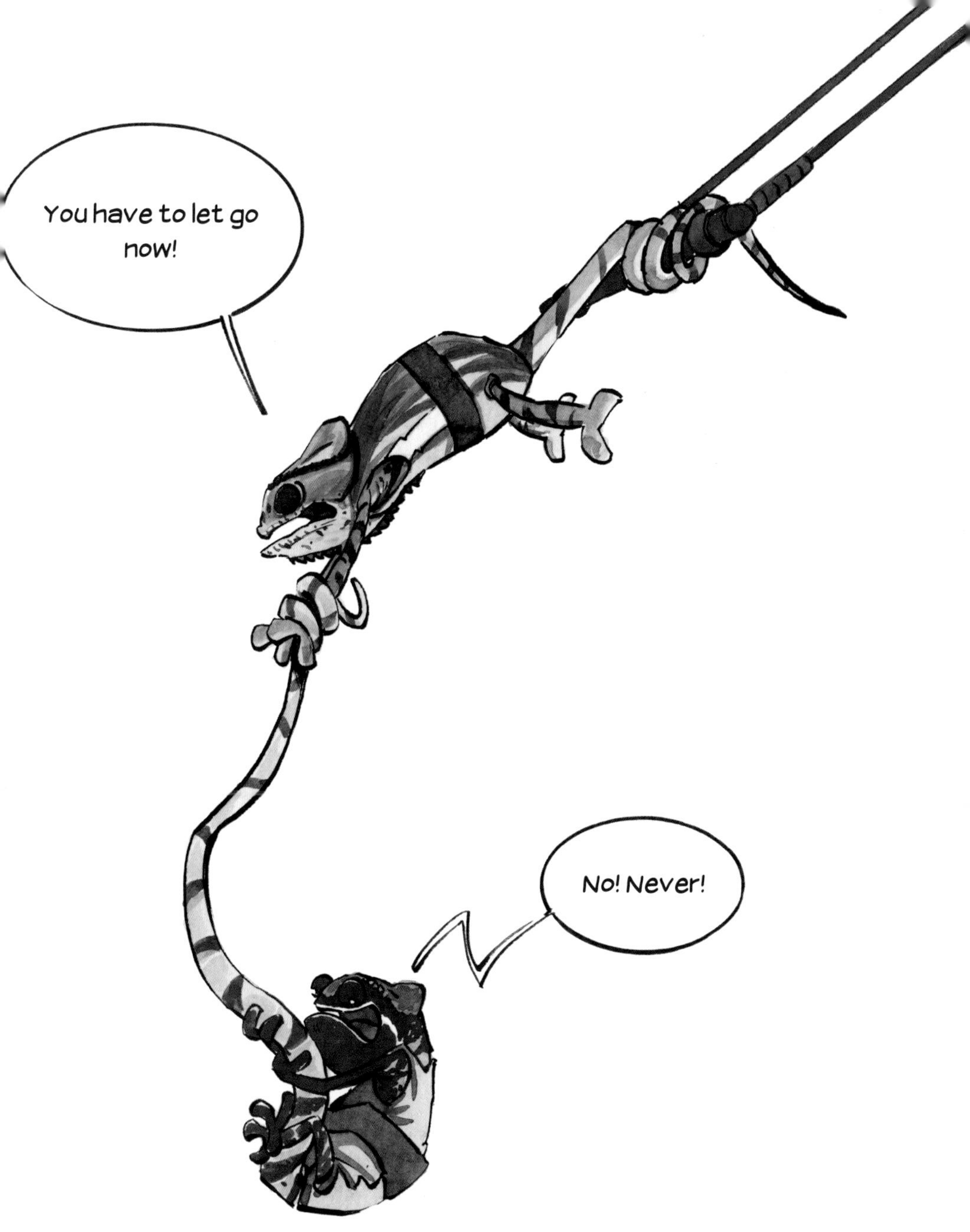
You have to let go now!
No! Never!

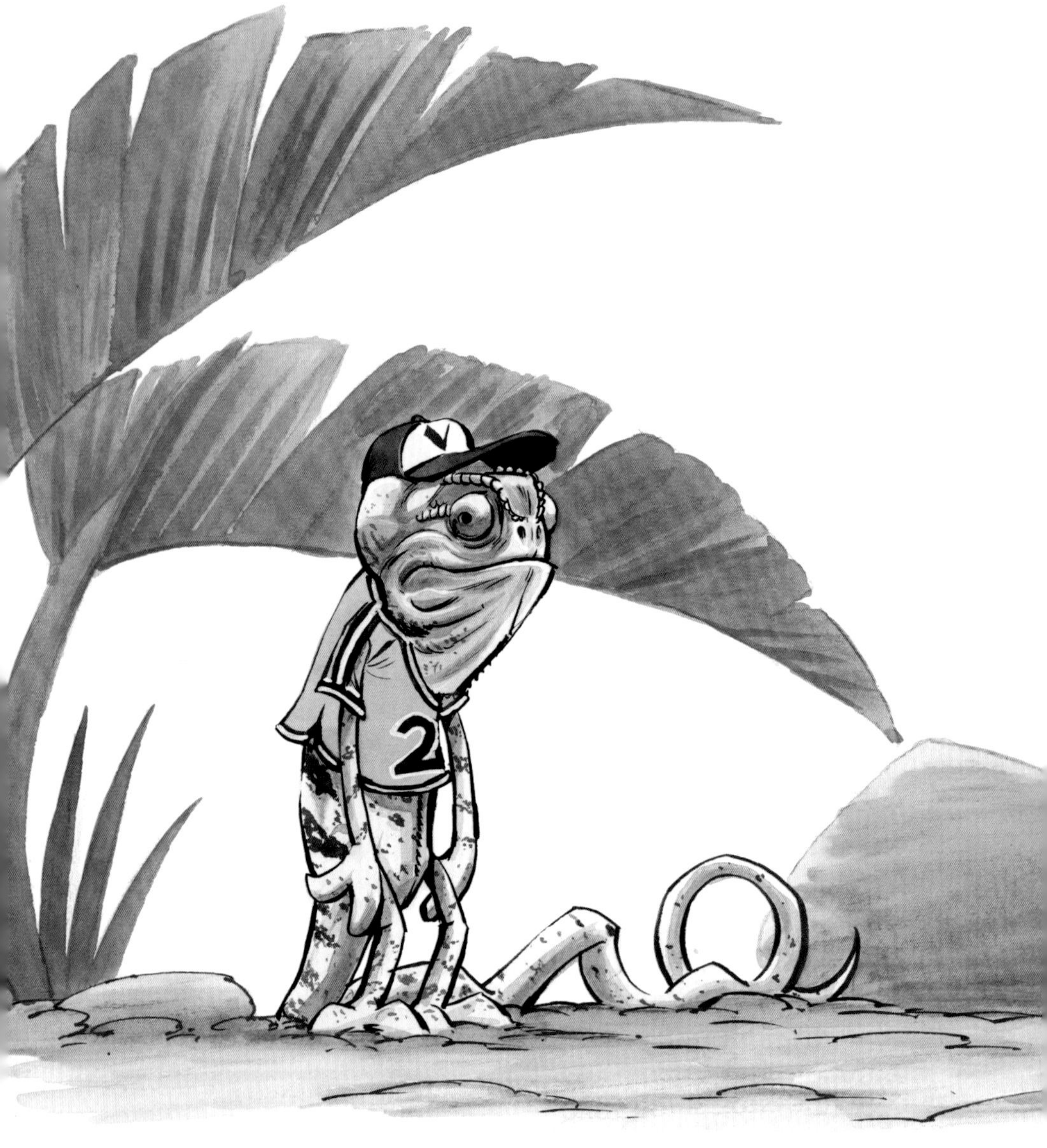

A chameleon's body is flattened sideways. This environmental adaptation helps the skilful acrobat to keep its balance while it moves among trees.

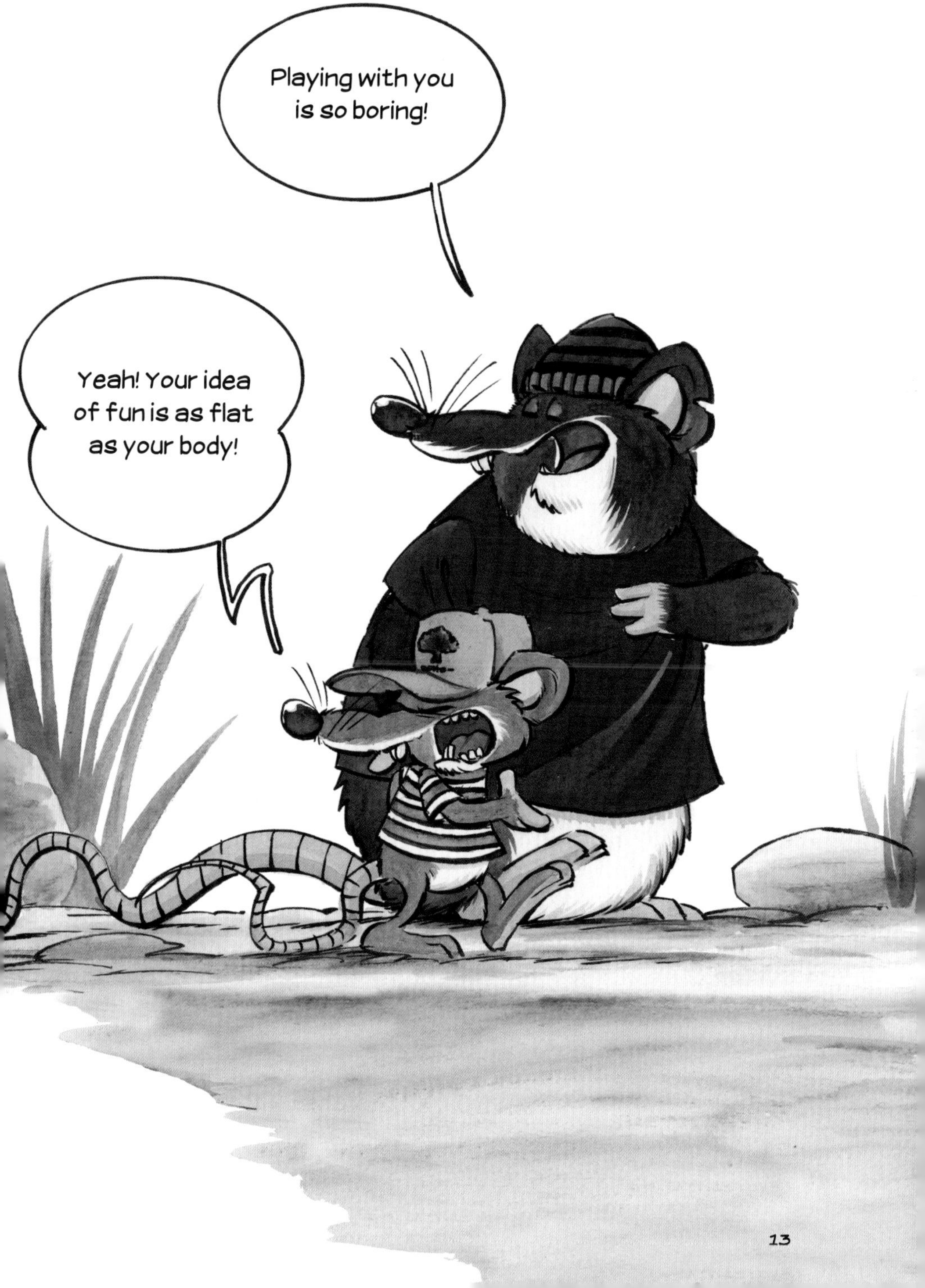
Playing with you is so boring!
Yeah! Your idea of fun is as flat as your body!

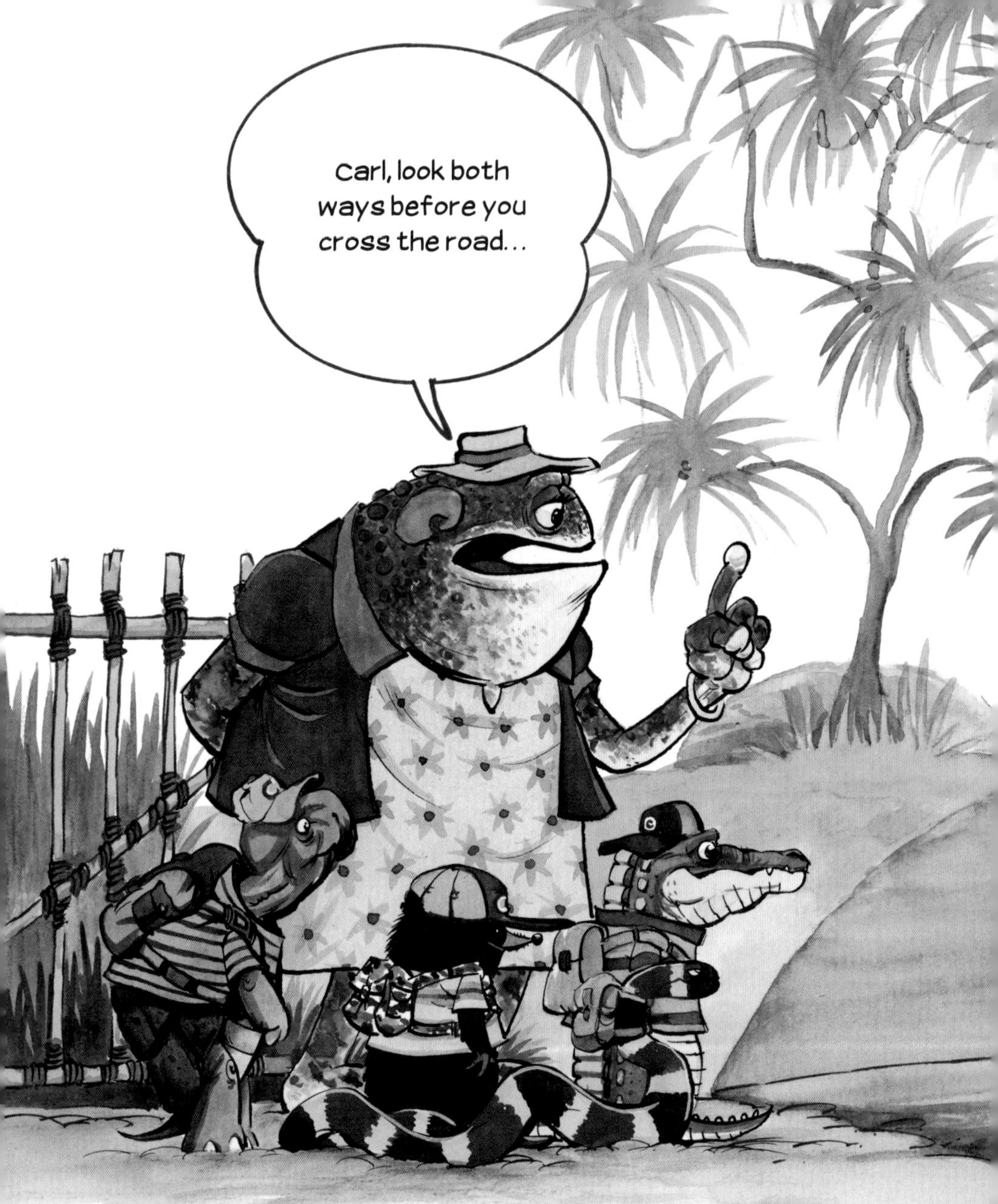
Carl, look both ways before you cross the road...

The chameleon's eyes can move independently of each other. One eye is capable of looking down at the ground while the other looks up at the sky.

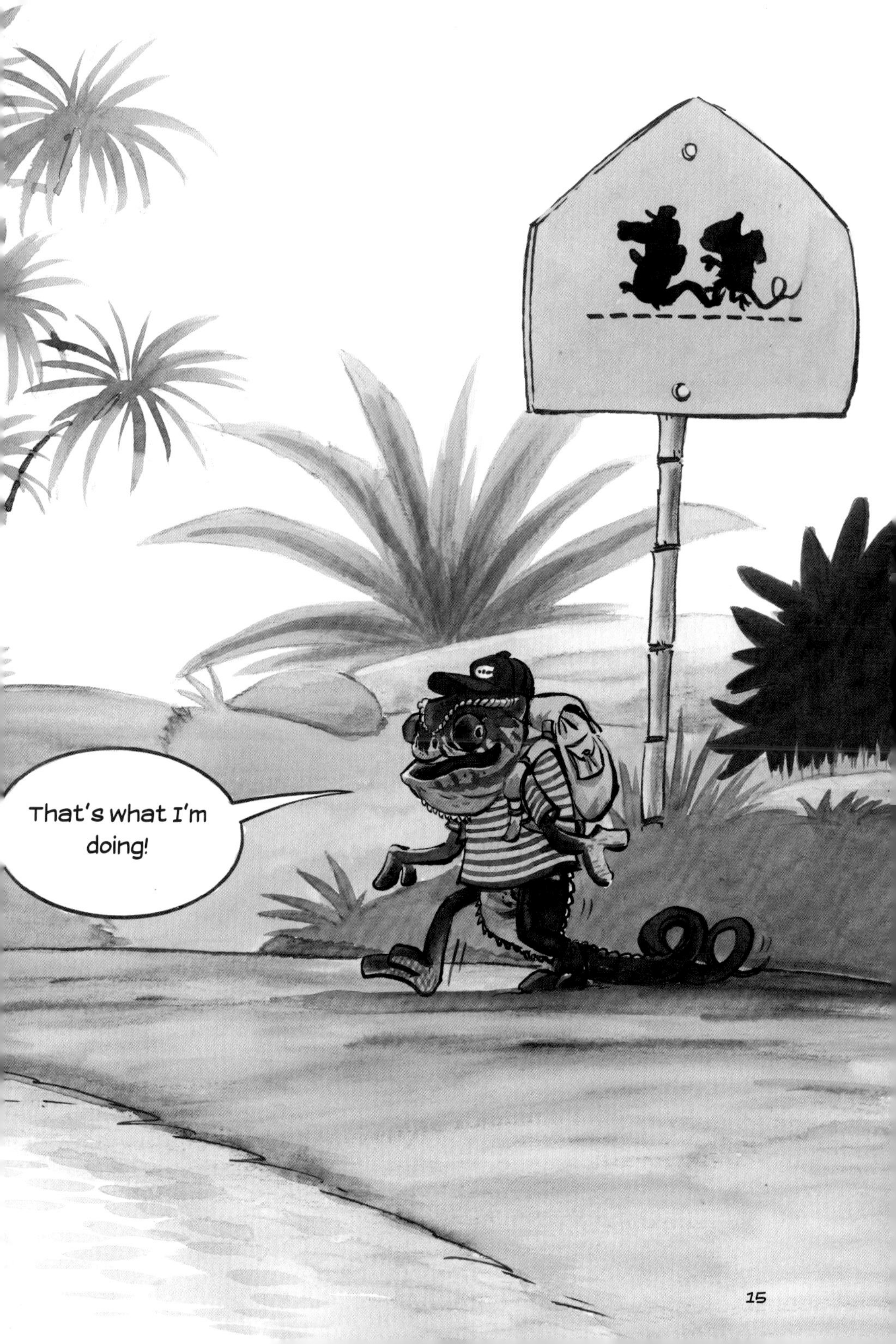
That's what I'm doing!

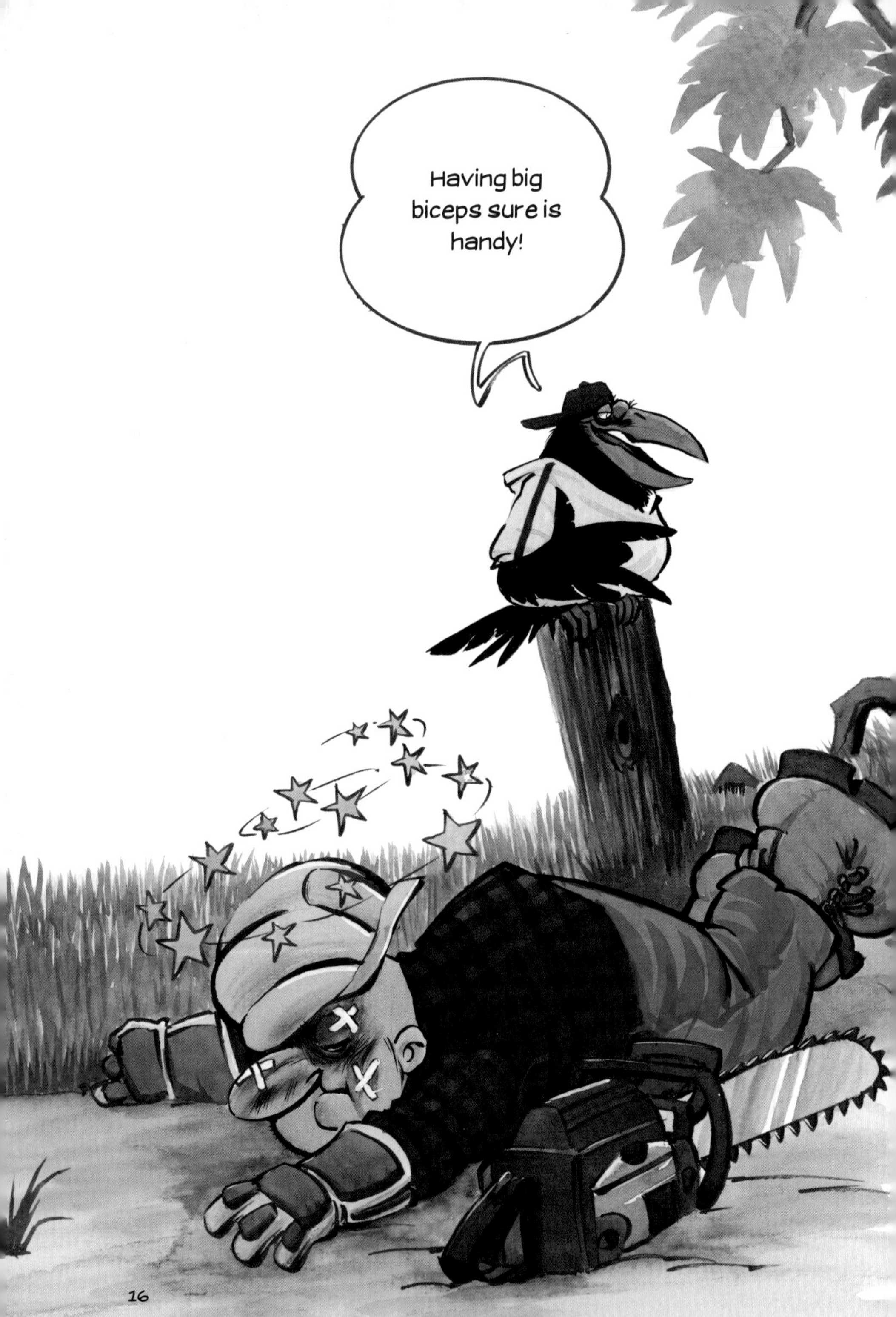
Having big biceps sure is handy!

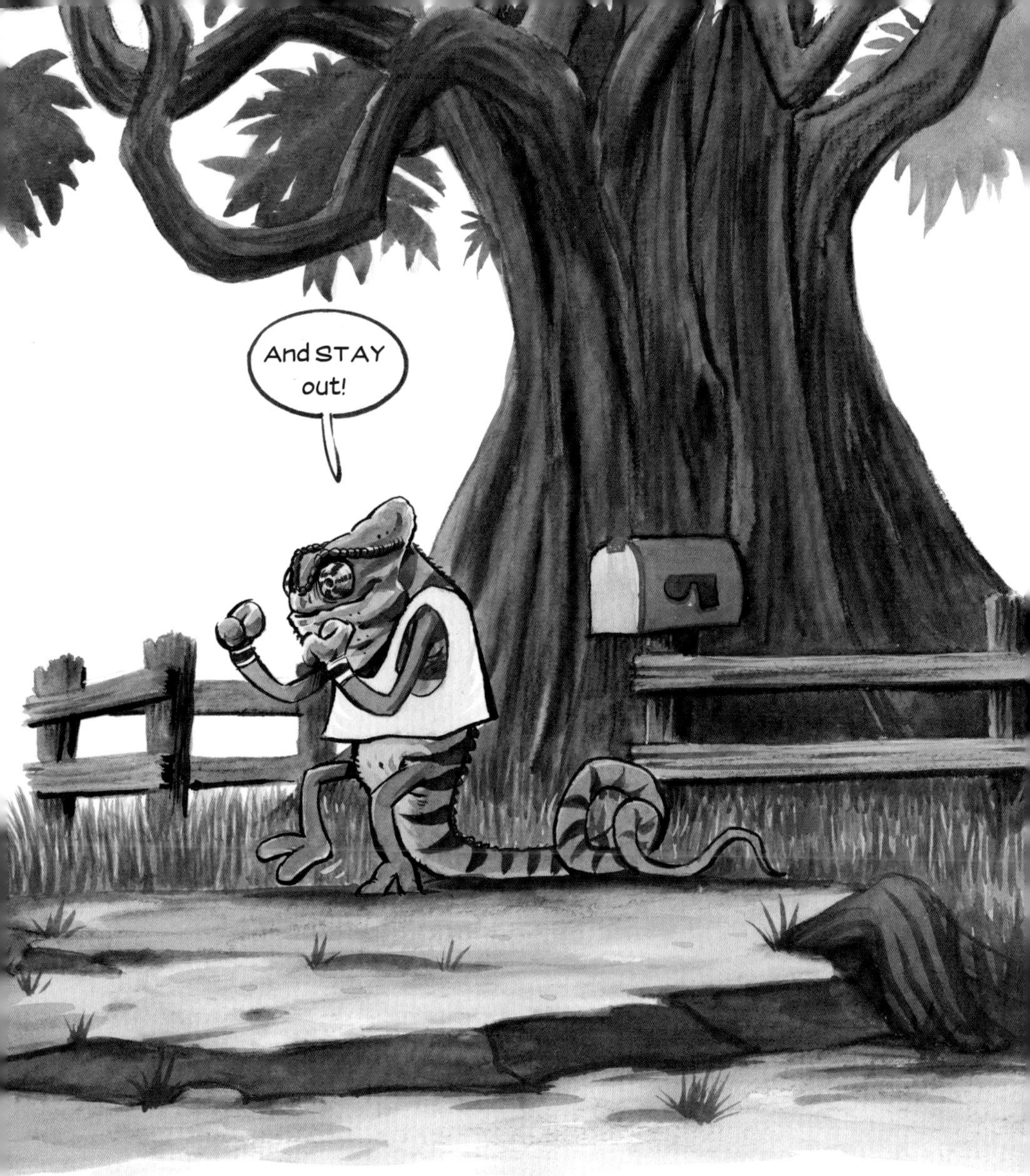
And STAY out!

In general, each chameleon adopts a tree, shrub or bush to build its shelter.

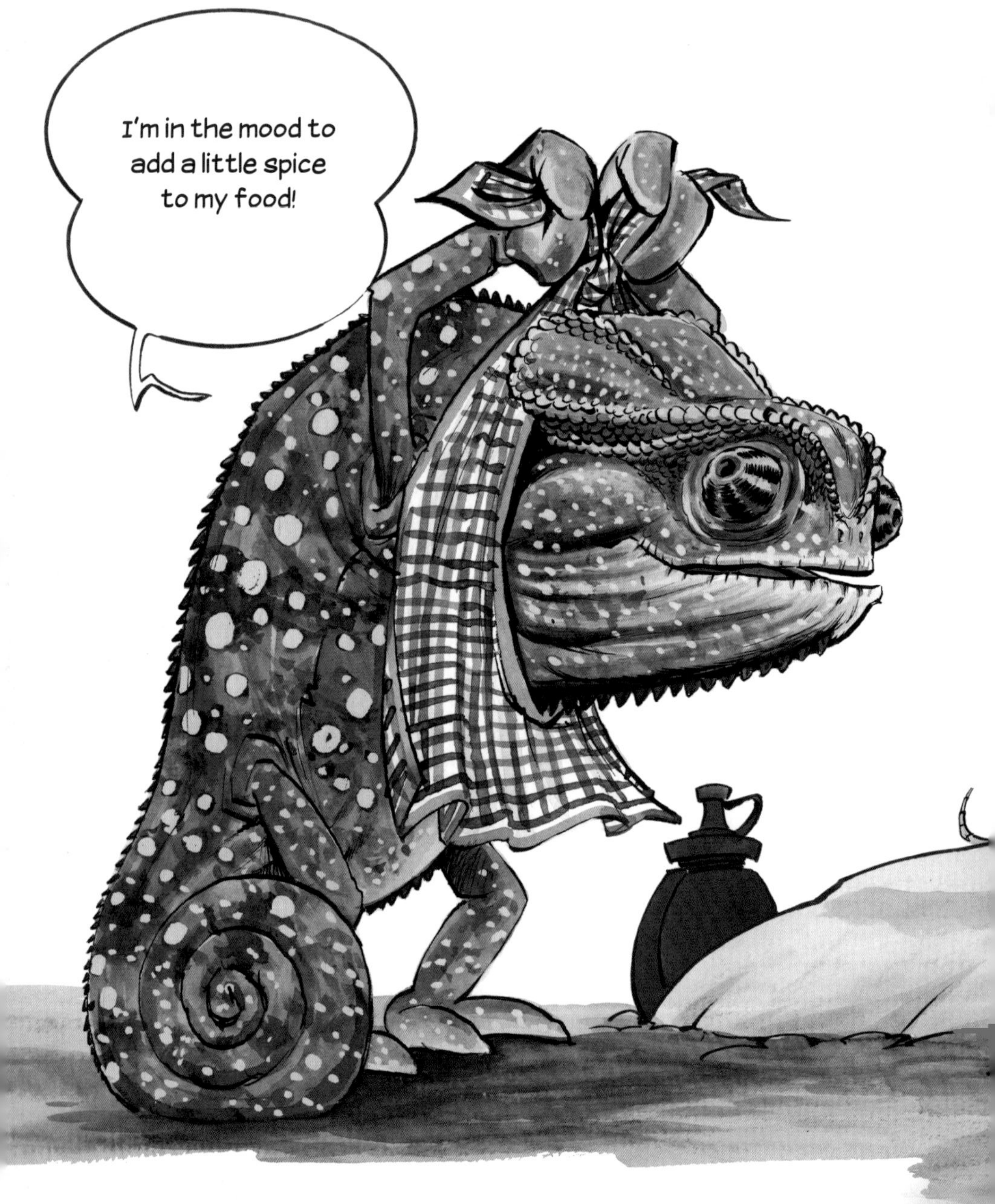
I'm in the mood to add a little spice to my food!

Chameleons mostly feed on insects and spiders. Some species also eat scorpions, birds, reptiles and small mammals.

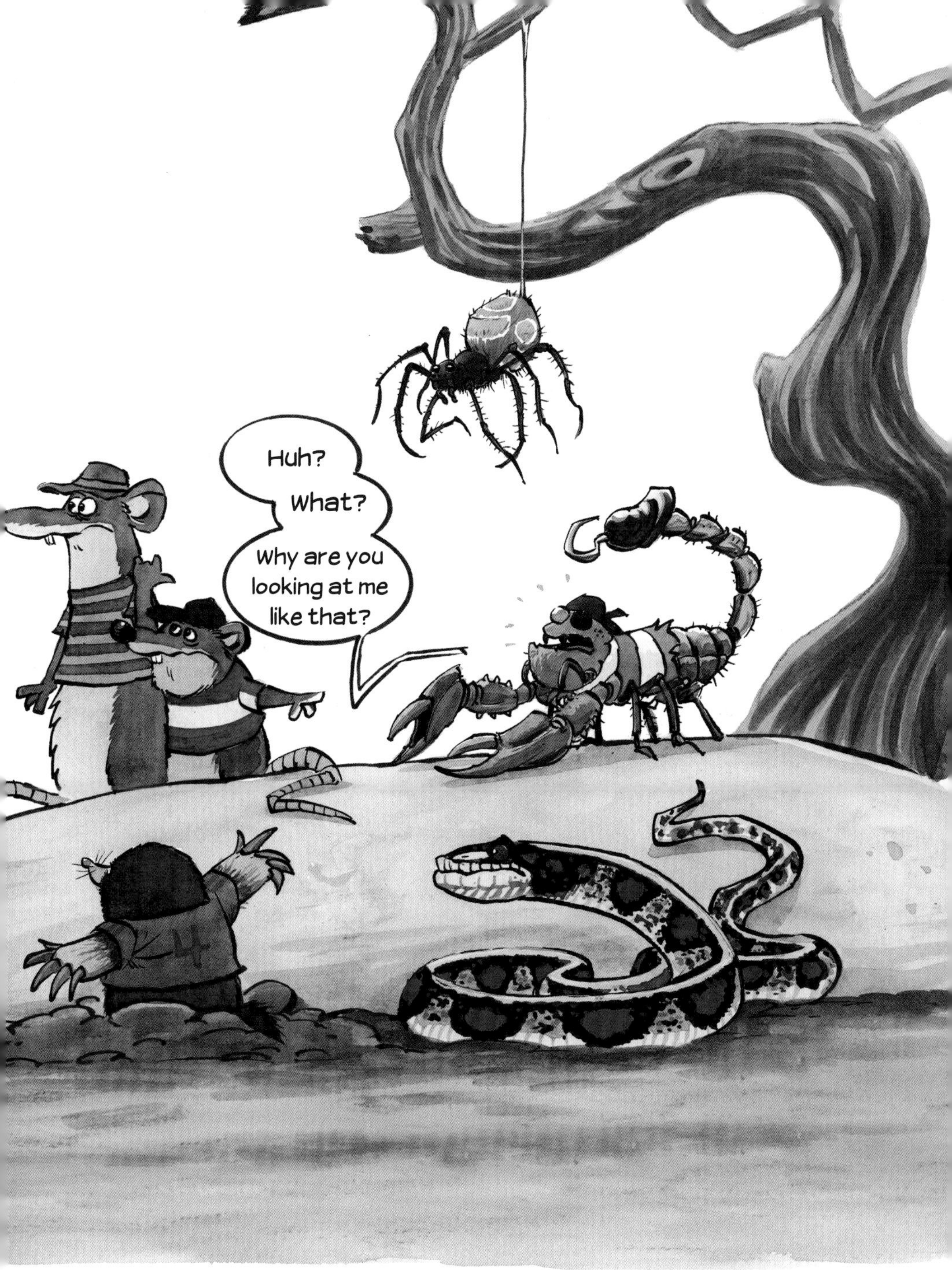
Huh?
What?
Why are you looking at me like that?

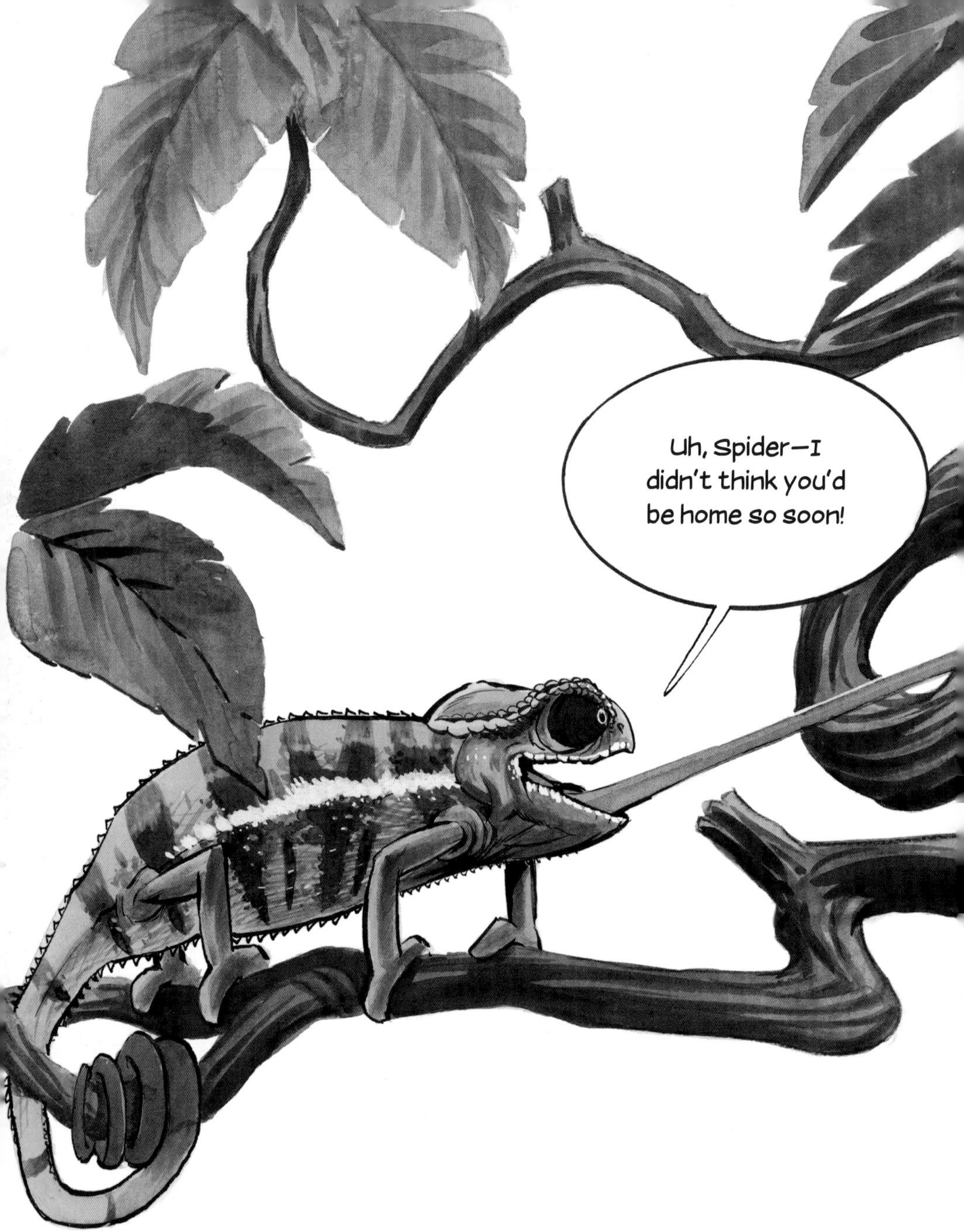
Uh, Spider—I didn't think you'd be home so soon!

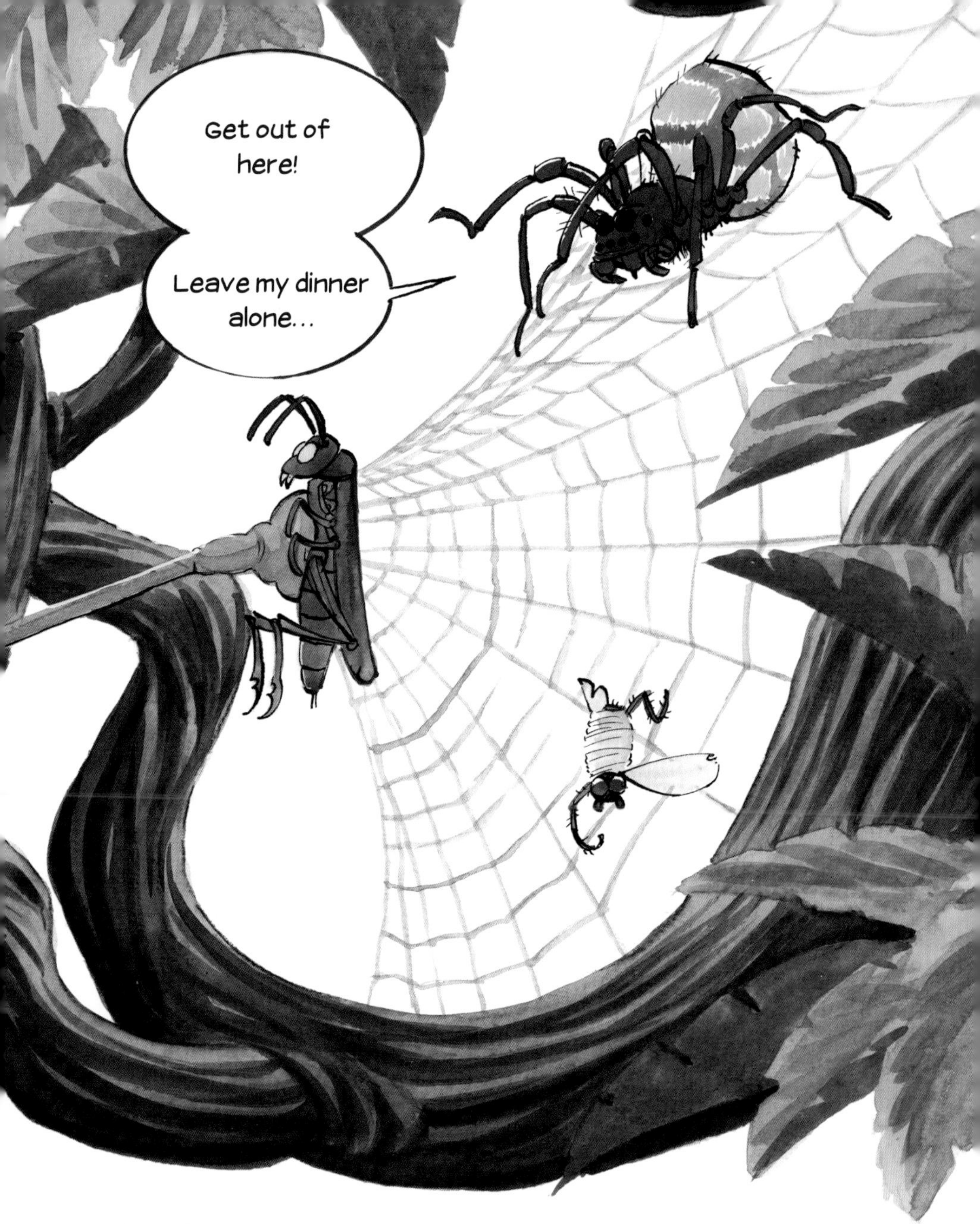
Get out of here!
Leave my dinner alone...

A chameleon lies in wait when it hunts. Motionless, it waits patiently for its prey to pass by. With great precision, its tongue then becomes a fatal weapon lashing out to eat the unsuspecting insect.

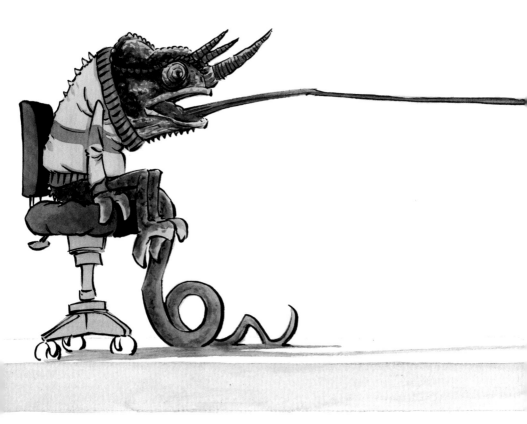

The chameleon's tongue, which resembles a long tube, is very extendable. Stretched, it is longer than the chameleon's head and body combined.

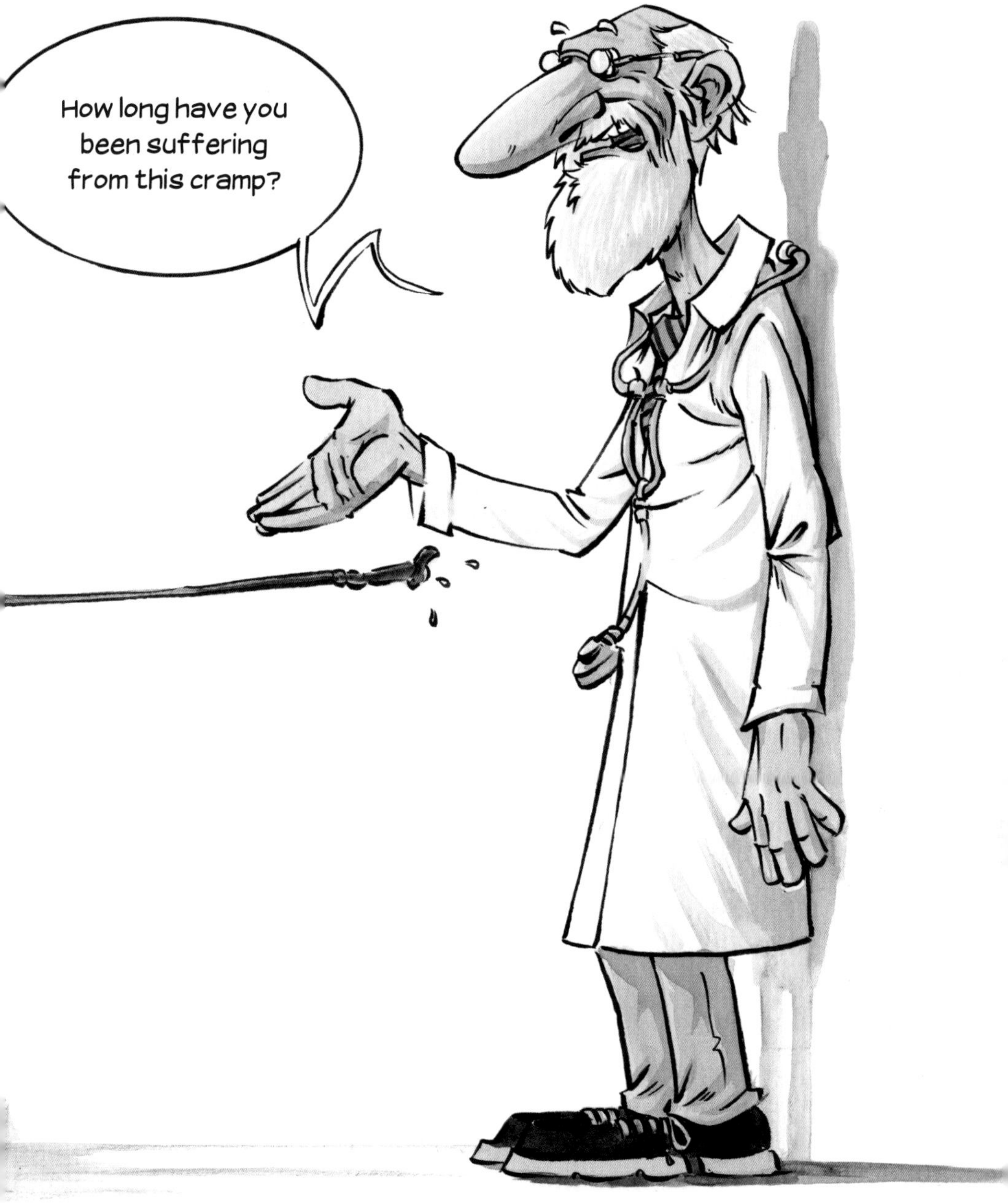
How long have you been suffering from this cramp?

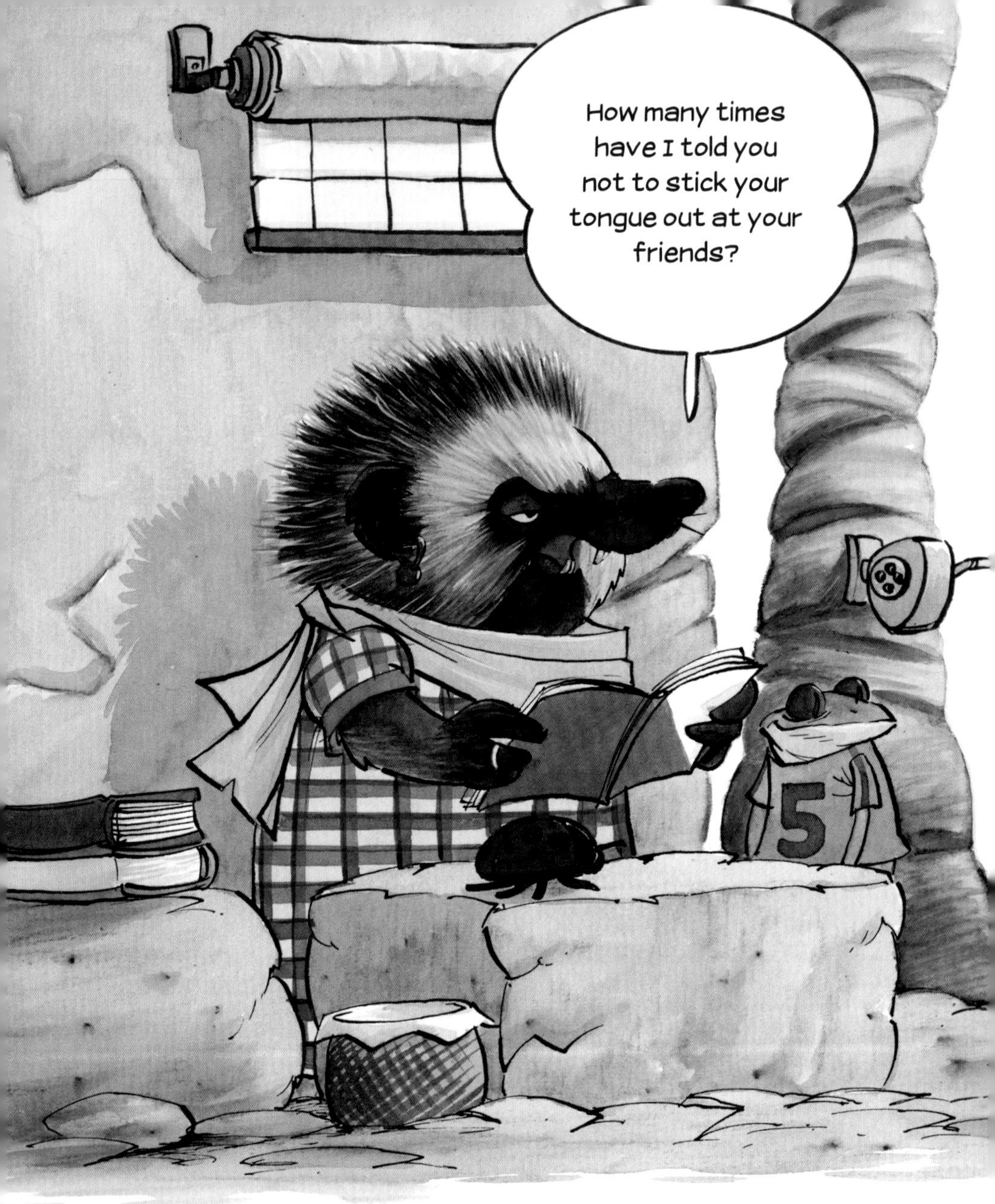
How many times have I told you not to stick your tongue out at your friends?
5

In its mouth, a chameleon's tongue is folded up like an accordion wrapped around a pointy bone. You could compare it to a compressed coil spring wrapped around a stick.

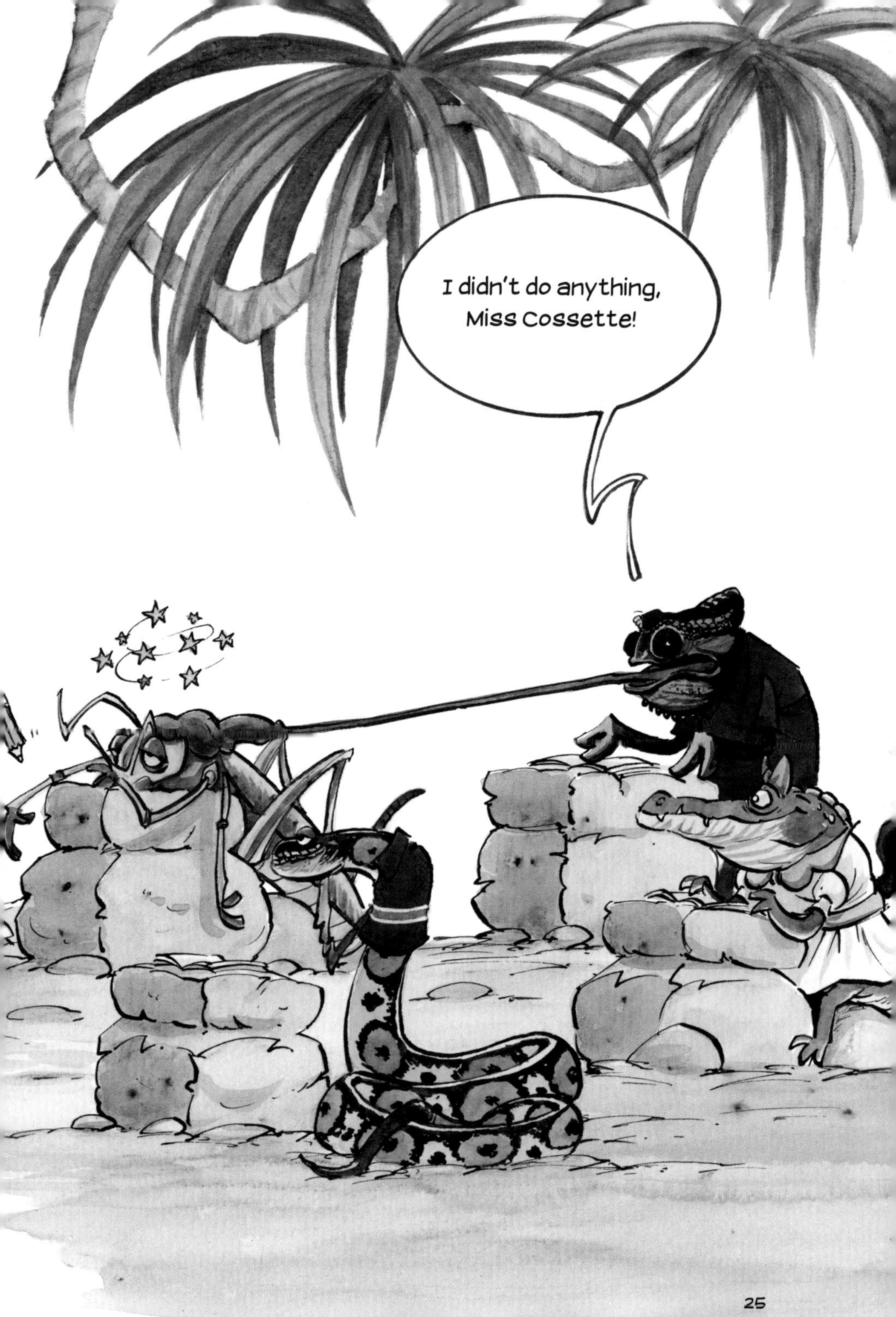
I didn't do anything, Miss Cossette!

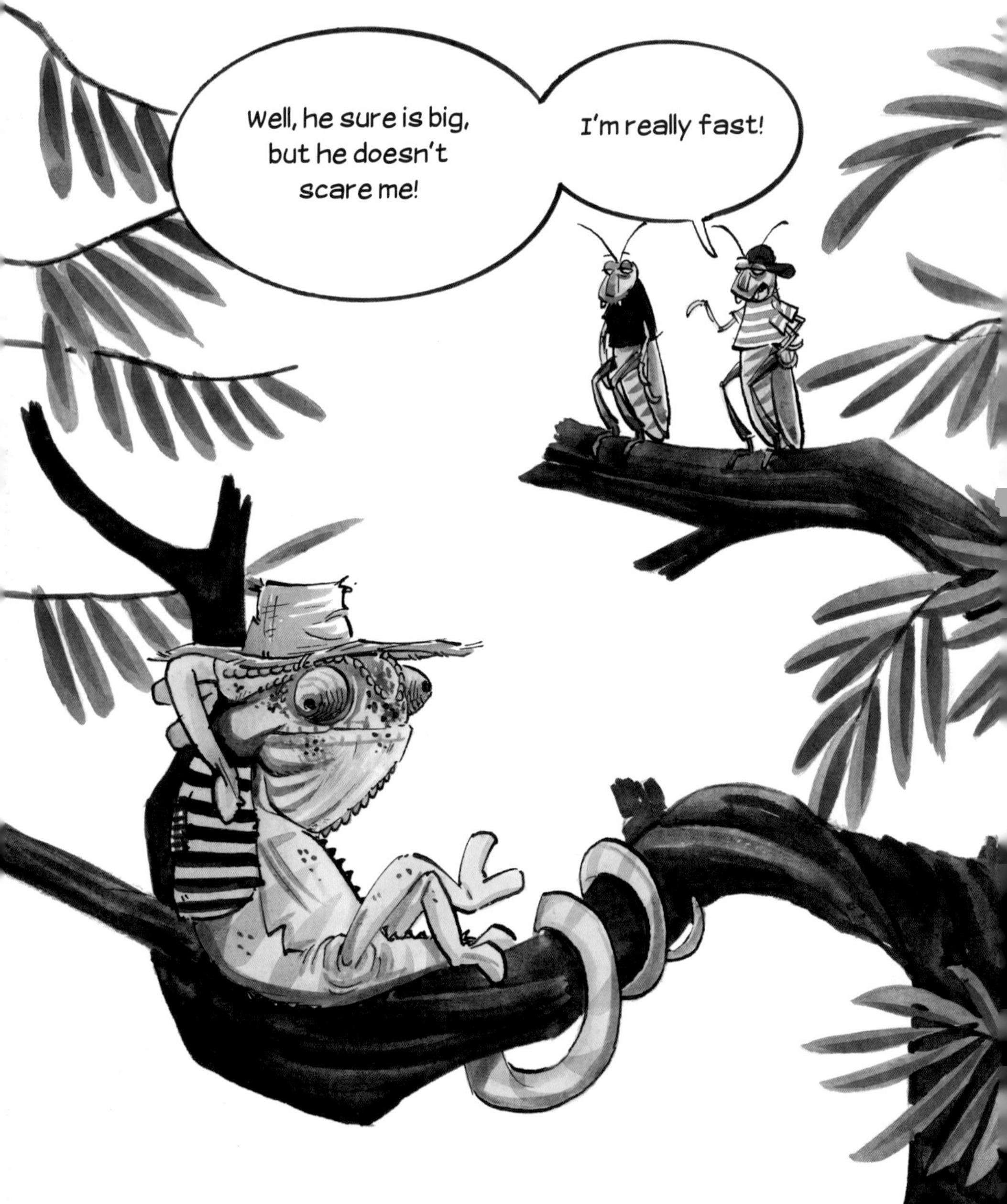
Well, he sure is big, but he doesn't scare me!
I'm really fast!

Like a released coil spring, the chameleon's tongue is propelled out at the powerful speed of 125th of a second. Its retraction back to the mouth takes about half a second.

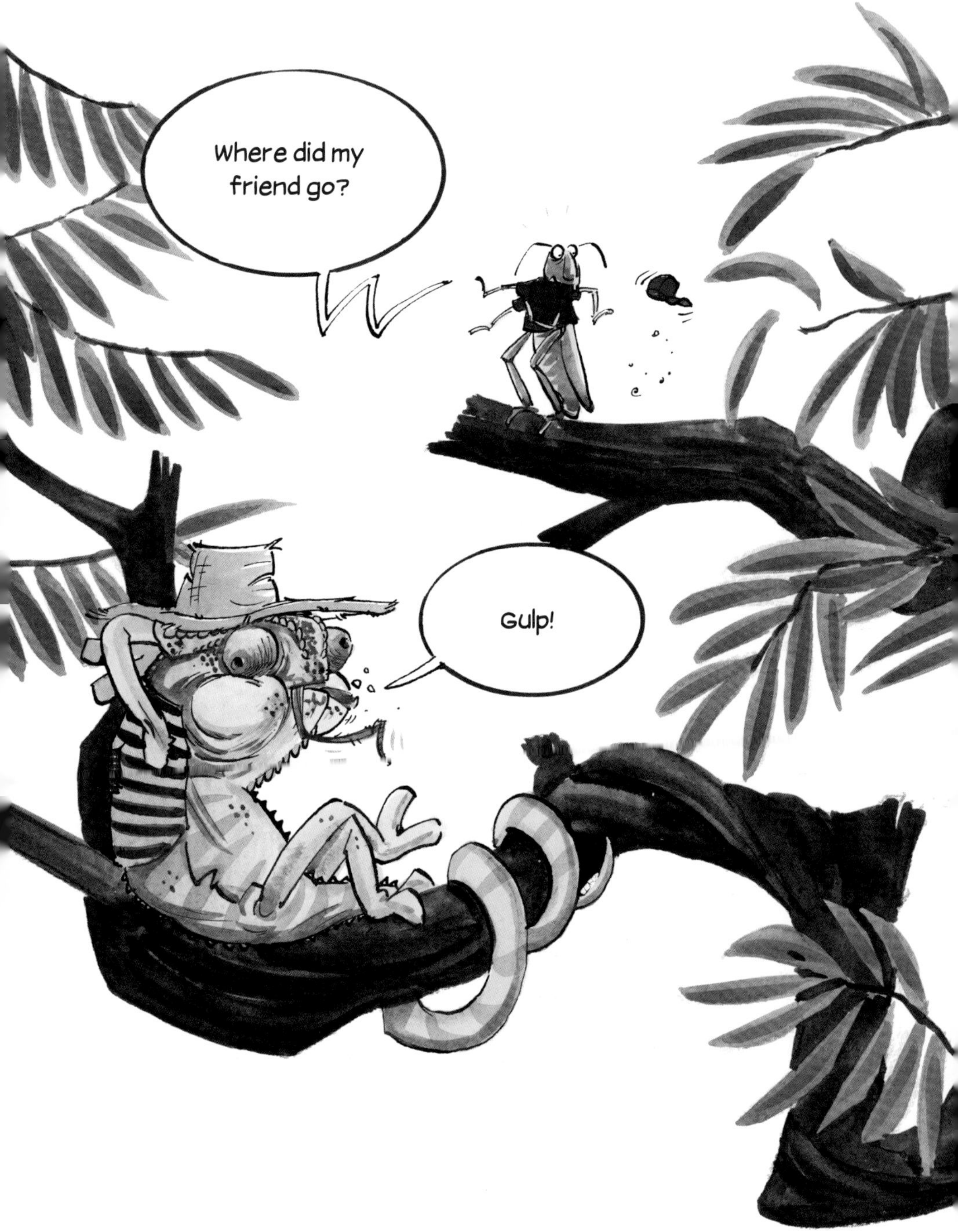
Where did my friend go?
Gulp!

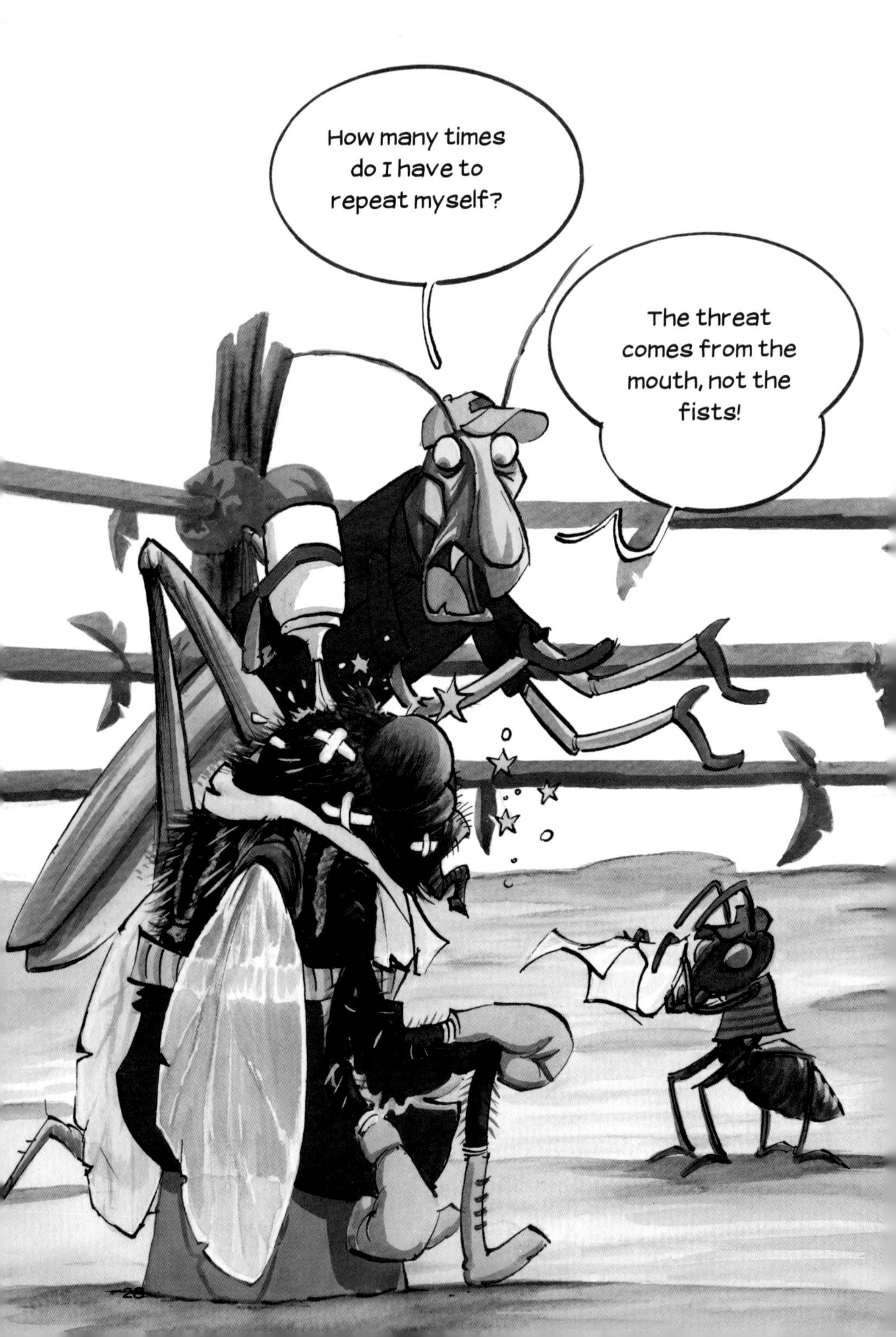
How many times do I have to repeat myself?
The threat comes from the mouth, not the fists!

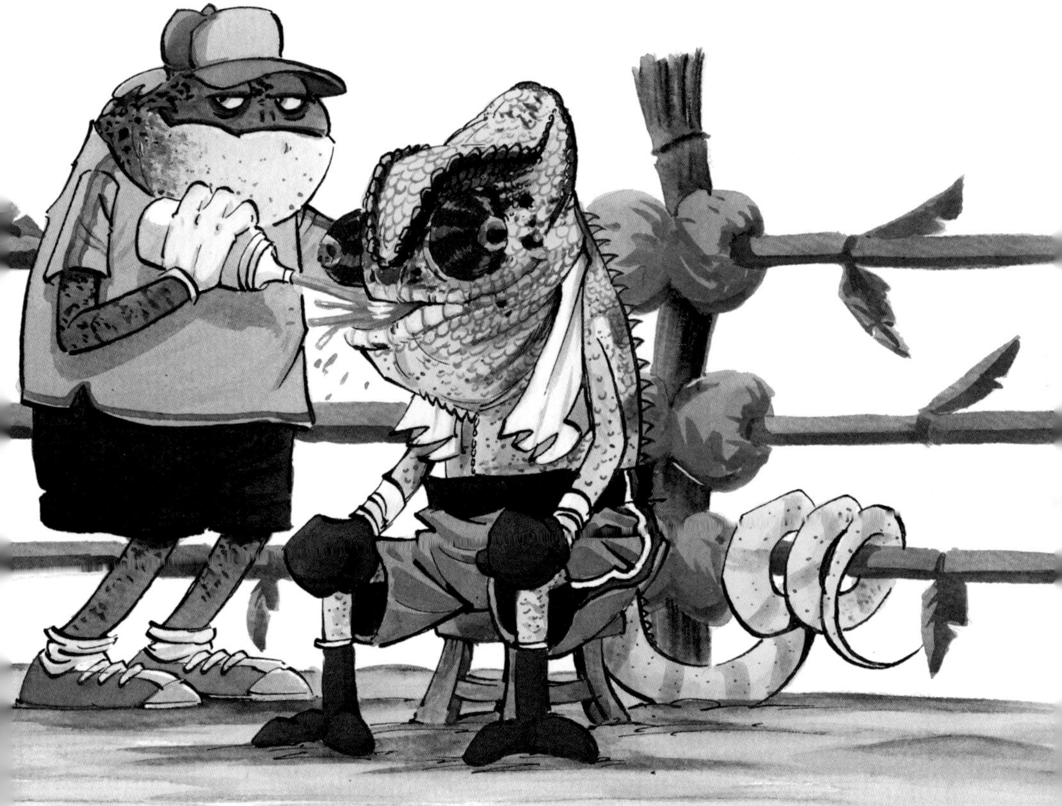

Once chameleons spot their **prey**, they knock it out with their club-shaped tongues.

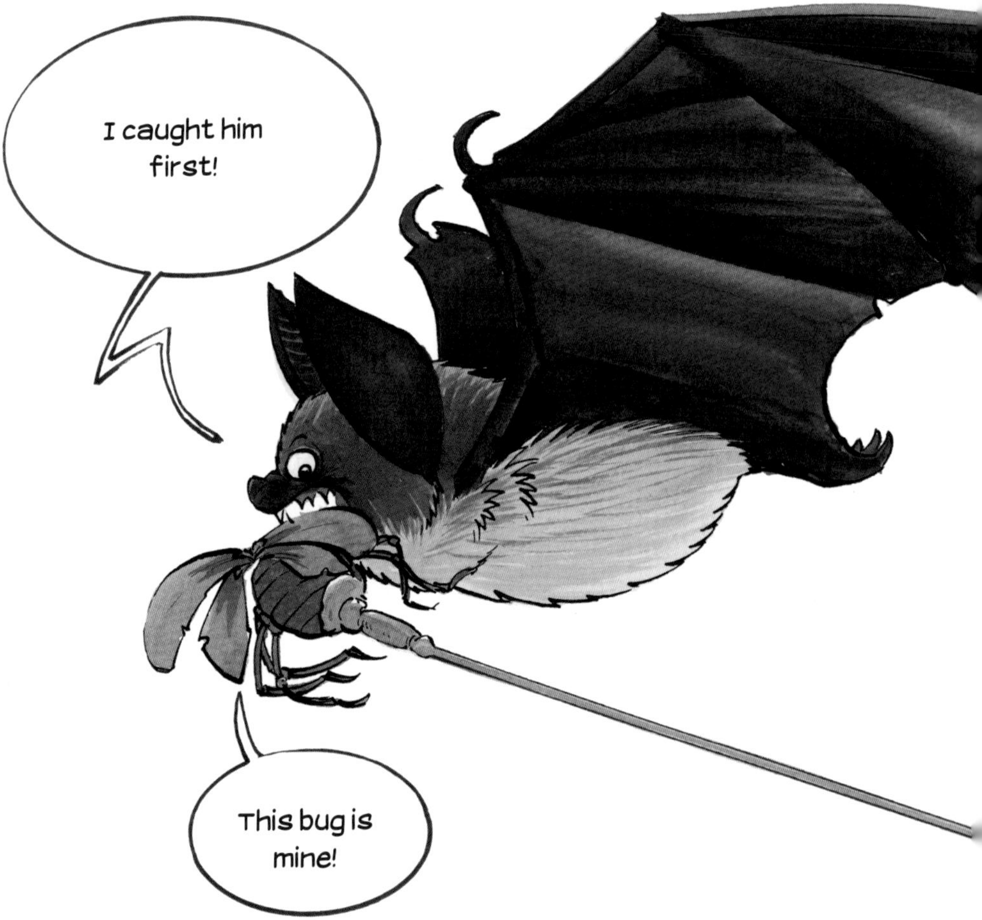
I caught him first!
This bug is mine!

A chameleon's tongue is coated with sticky saliva, which firmly holds onto the insect so the chameleon can bring it to its mouth to eat.

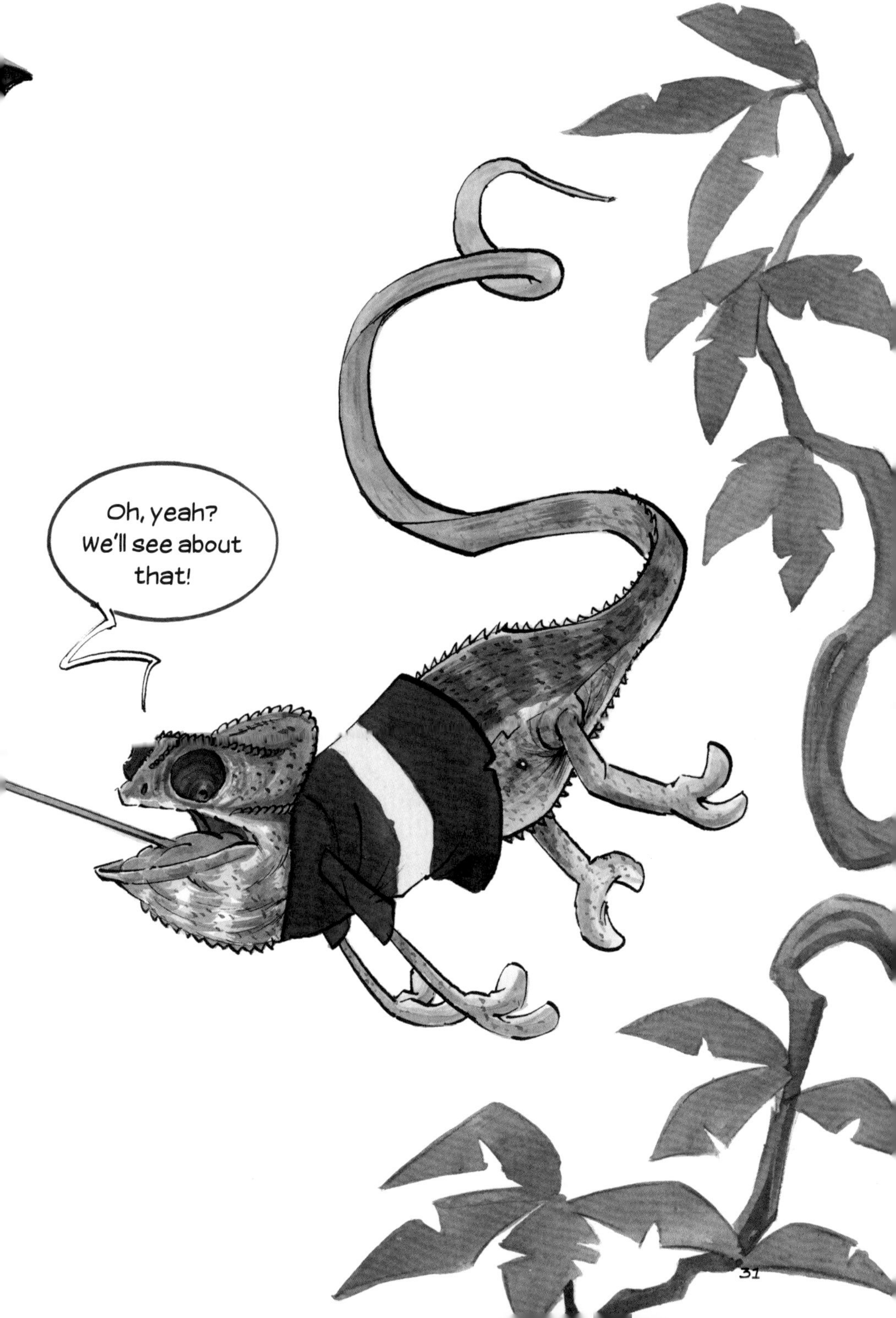
Oh, yeah? We'll see about that!

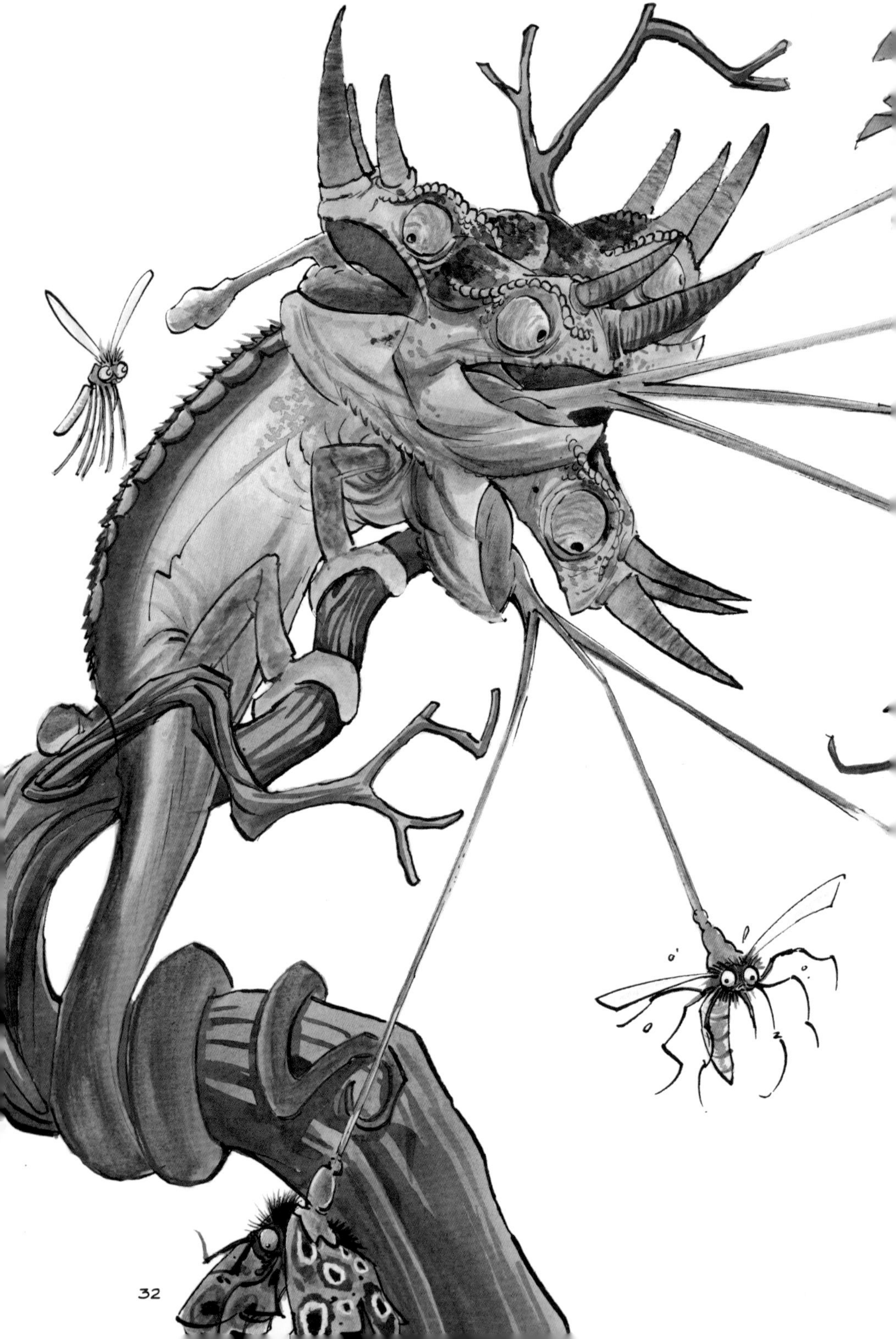

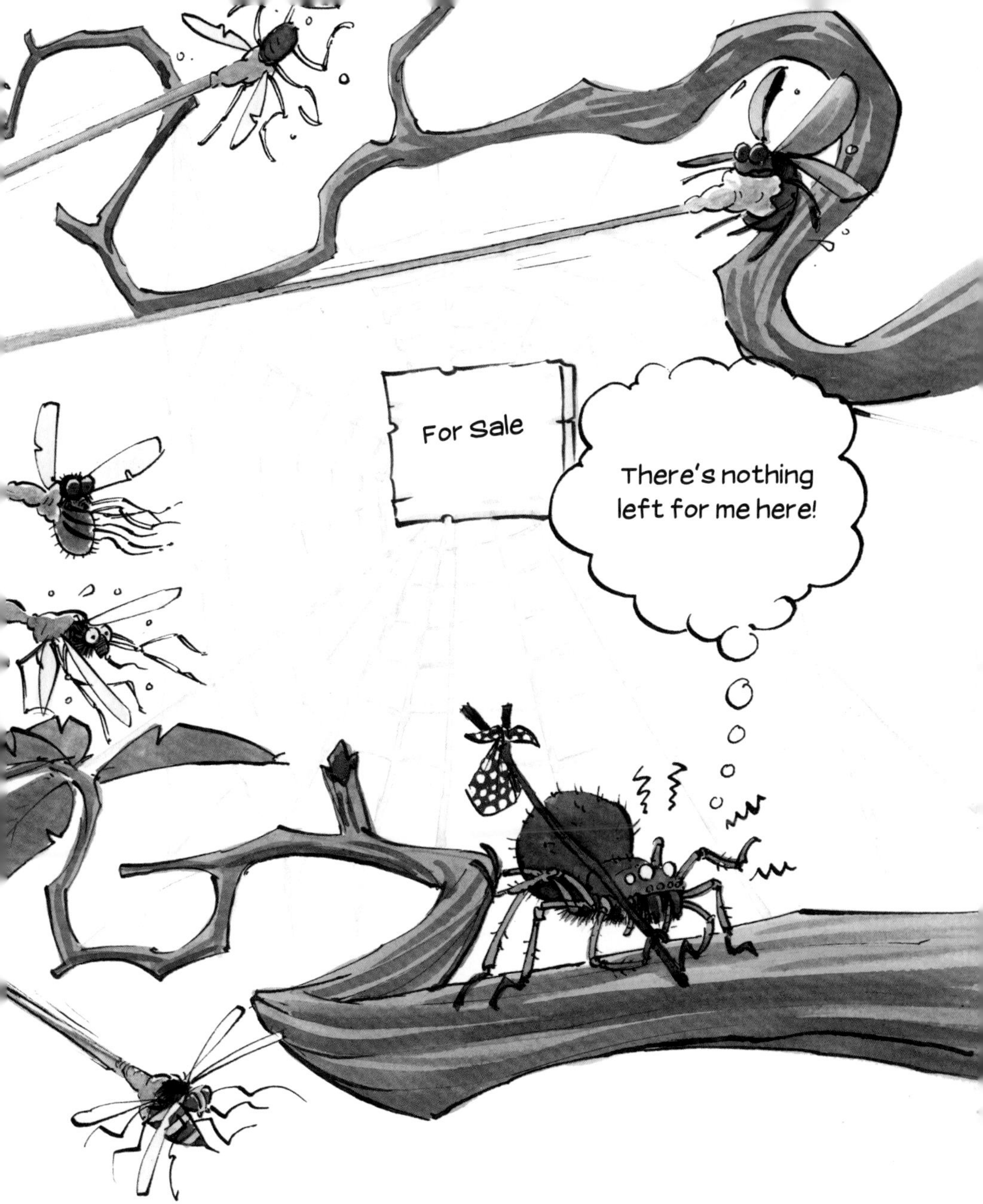
For Sale
There's nothing left for me here!

A chameleon can catch a hundred flying insects with its tongue in as little as a few minutes.

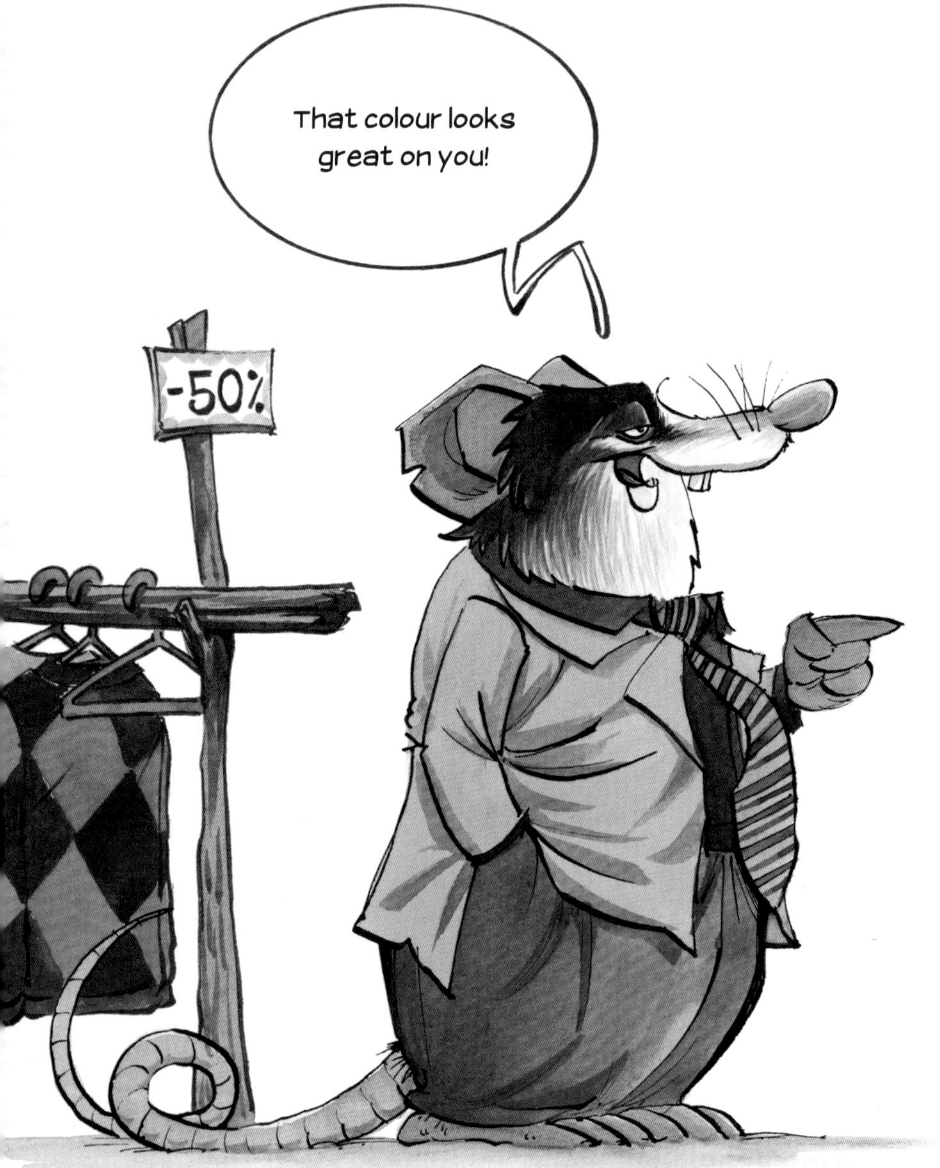
That colour looks great on you!
-50%

Chameleons have the ability to change colours in just a few seconds.

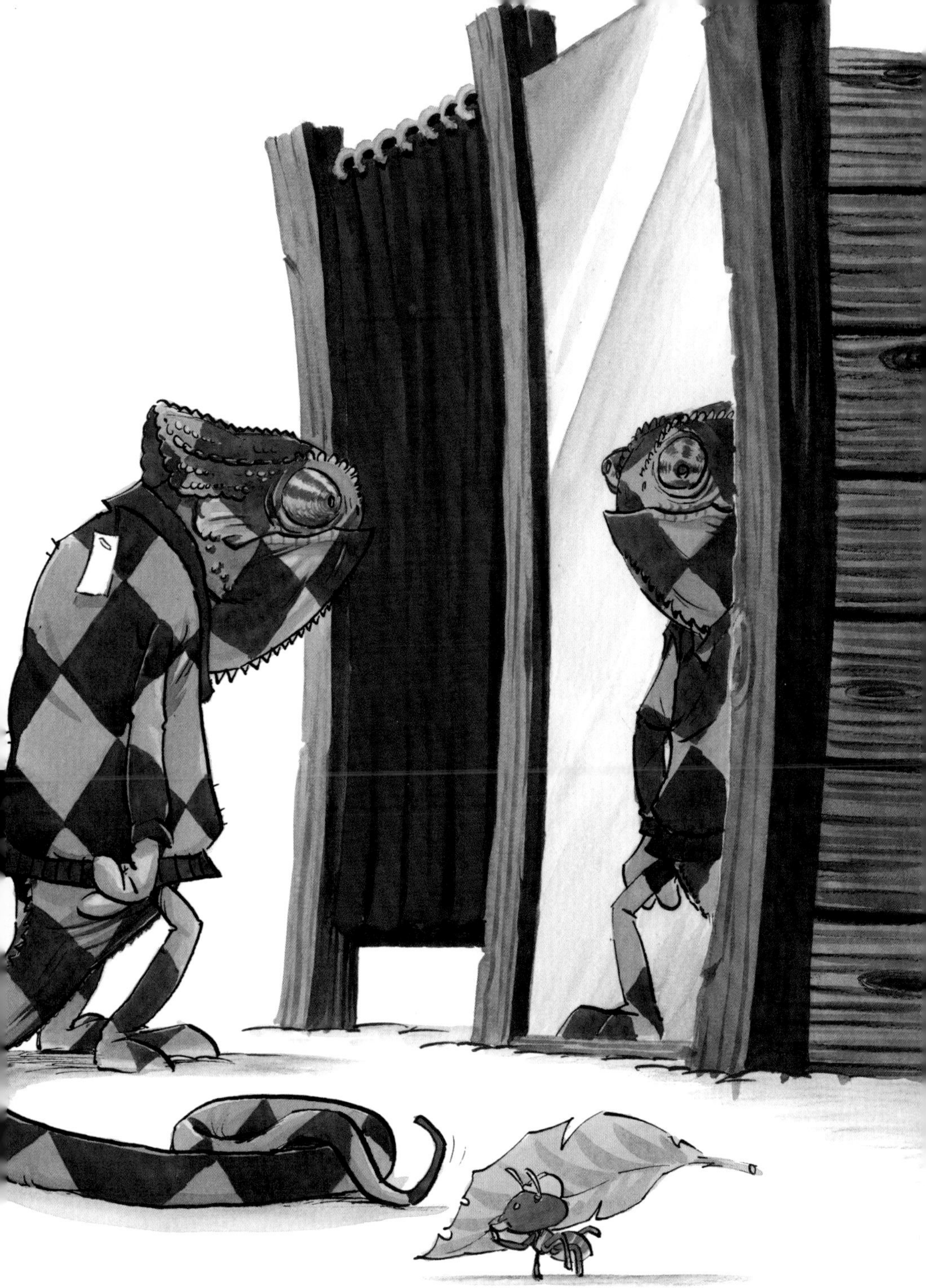

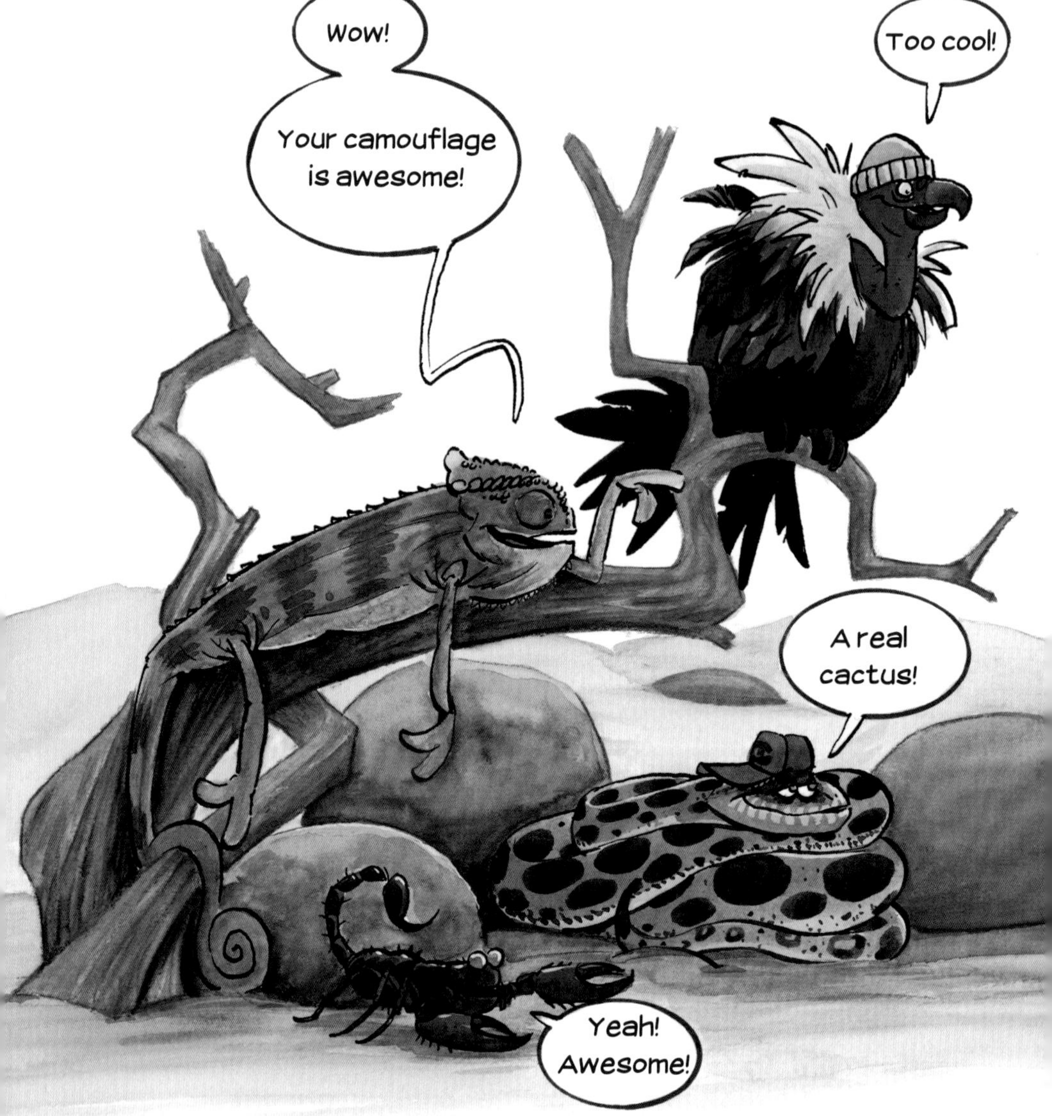
Wow!
Your camouflage is awesome!
Too cool!
A real cactus!
Yeah! Awesome!

Depending on a chameleon's environment, its colours can vary greatly from one species to another.

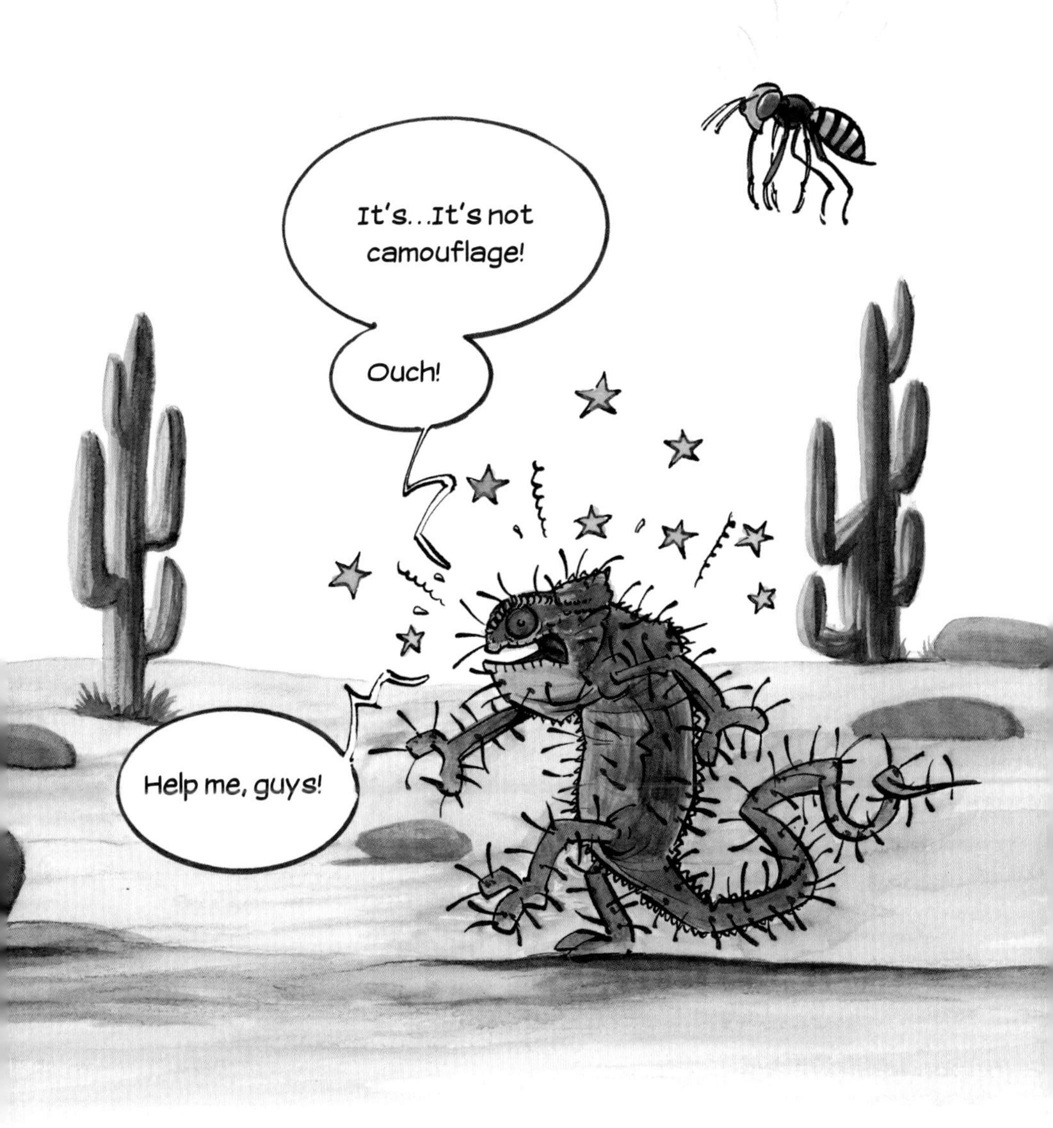
It's...It's not camouflage!
Ouch!
Help me, guys!

Desert chameleons only use bland colours similar to those of sand and rocks to blend into their surroundings.

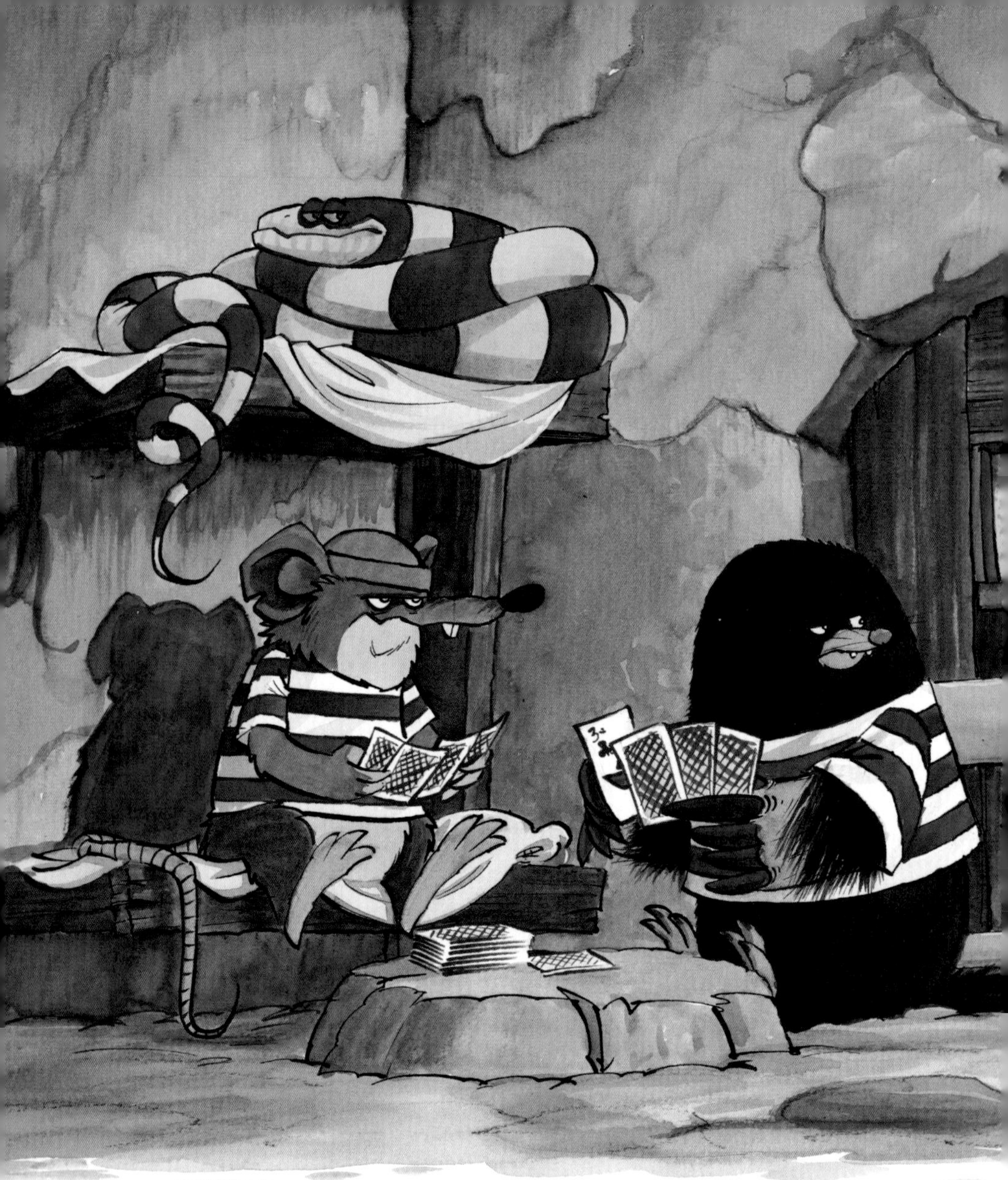

It's thanks to its skin cells that the chameleon's colour variation is possible. These cells react to heat and light, as well as the animal's emotions.

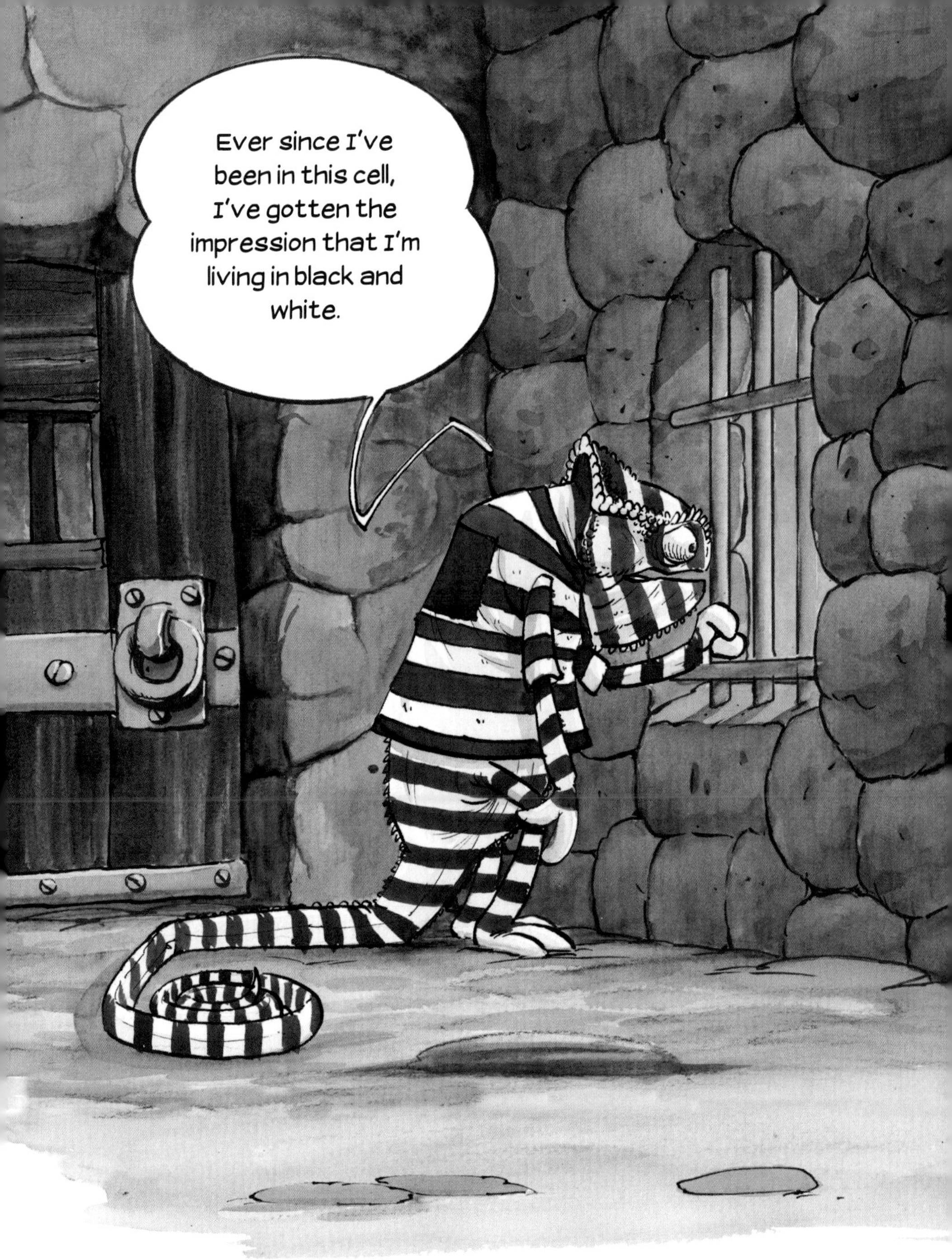
Ever since I've been in this cell, I've gotten the impression that I'm living in black and white.

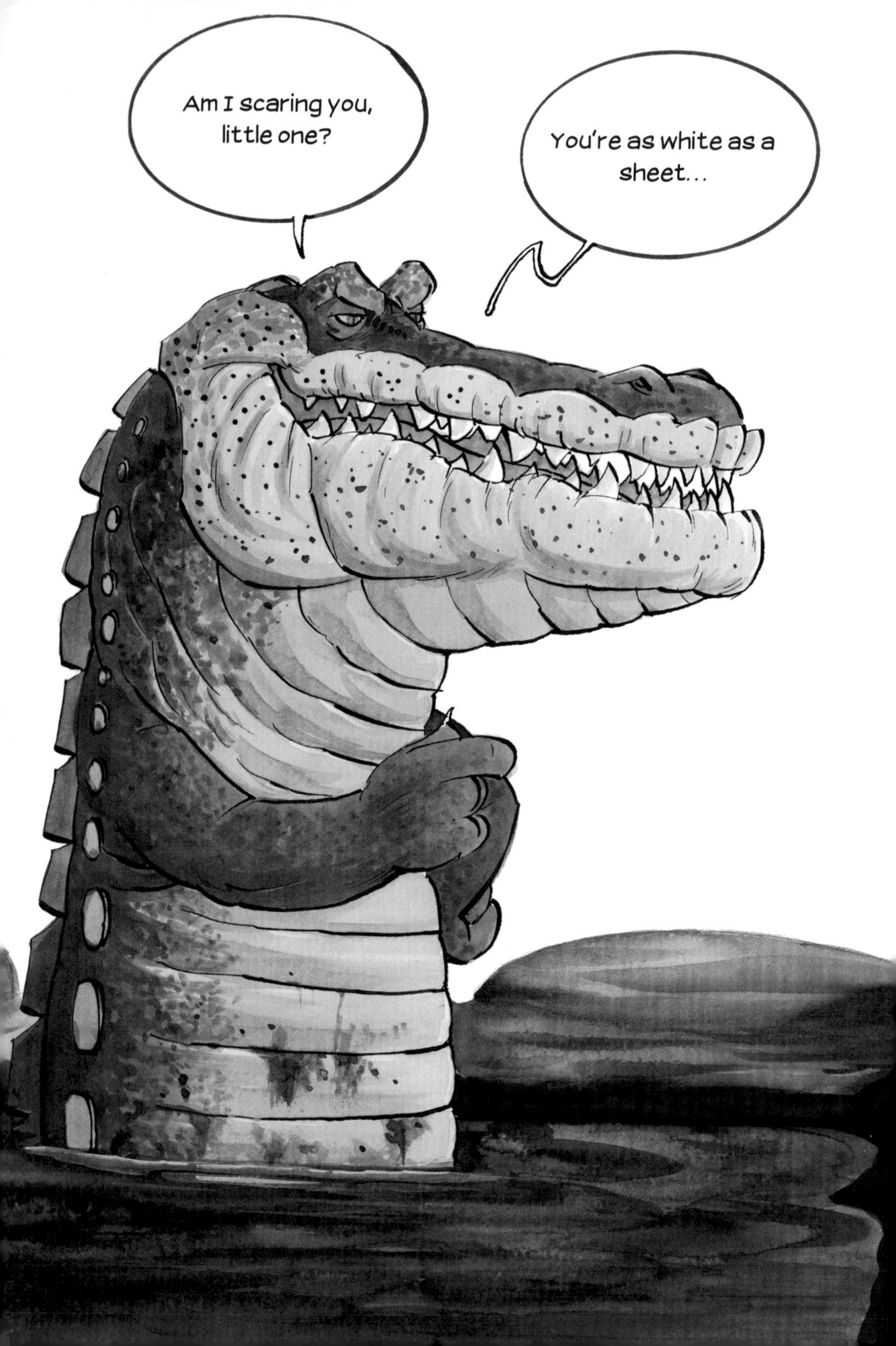
Am I scaring you, little one?
You're as white as a sheet...

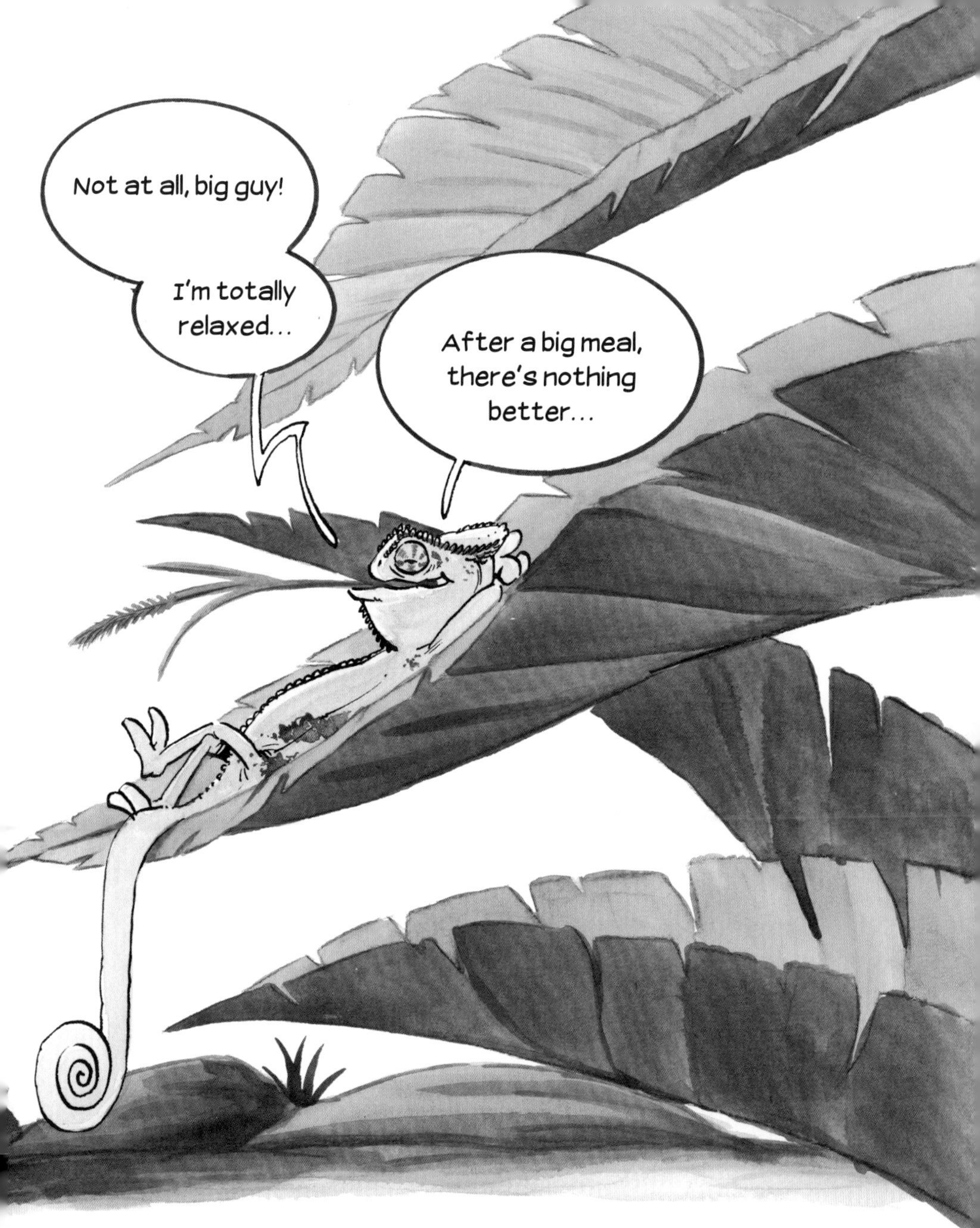
Not at all, big guy!
I'm totally relaxed…
After a big meal, there's nothing better…

Chameleons lose their colours when they're scared, relaxing or digesting.

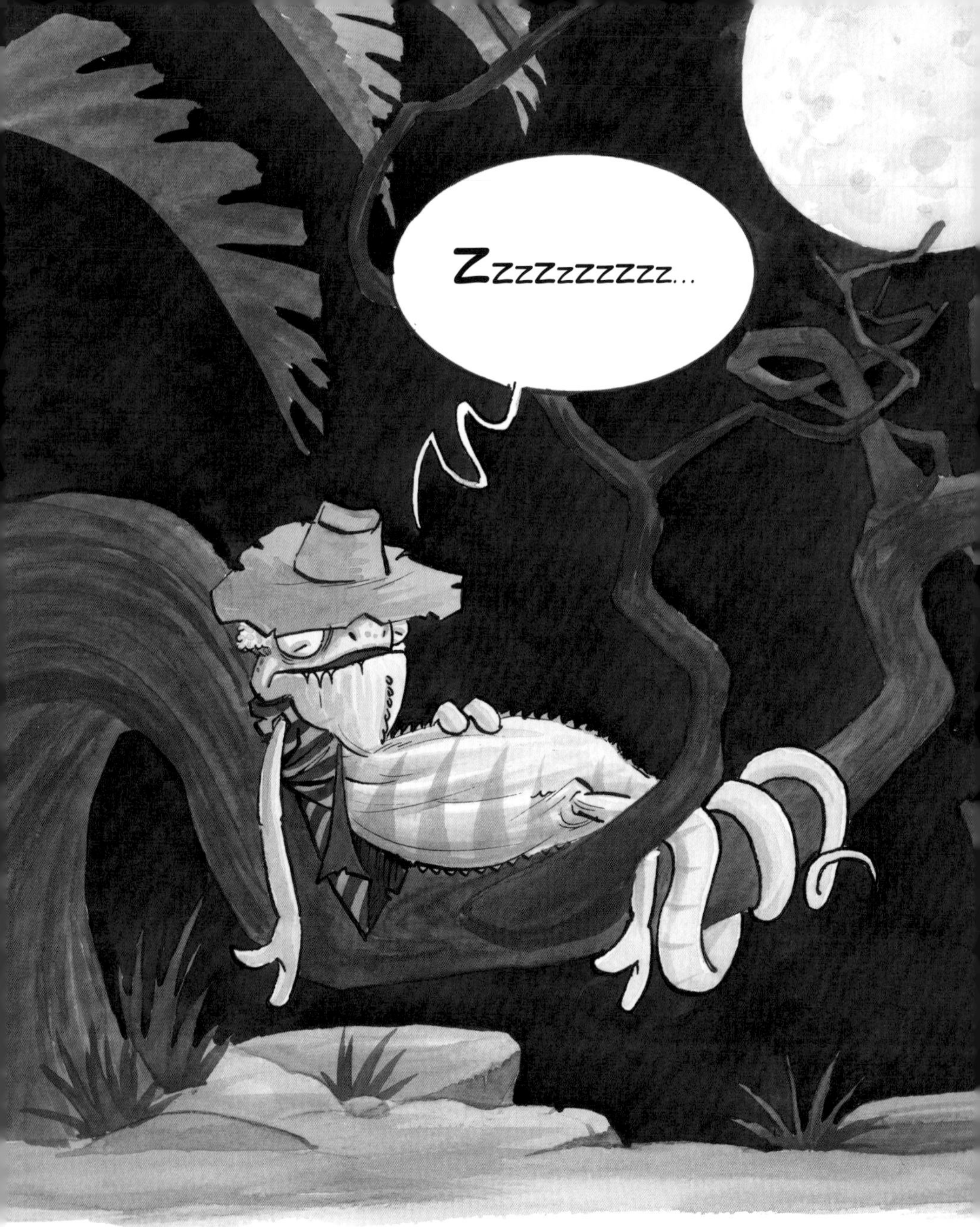
Zzzzzzzzzz...

Chameleons turn pale while they sleep at night. On the other hand, their colours darken to absorb the sun's rays and heat during the day.

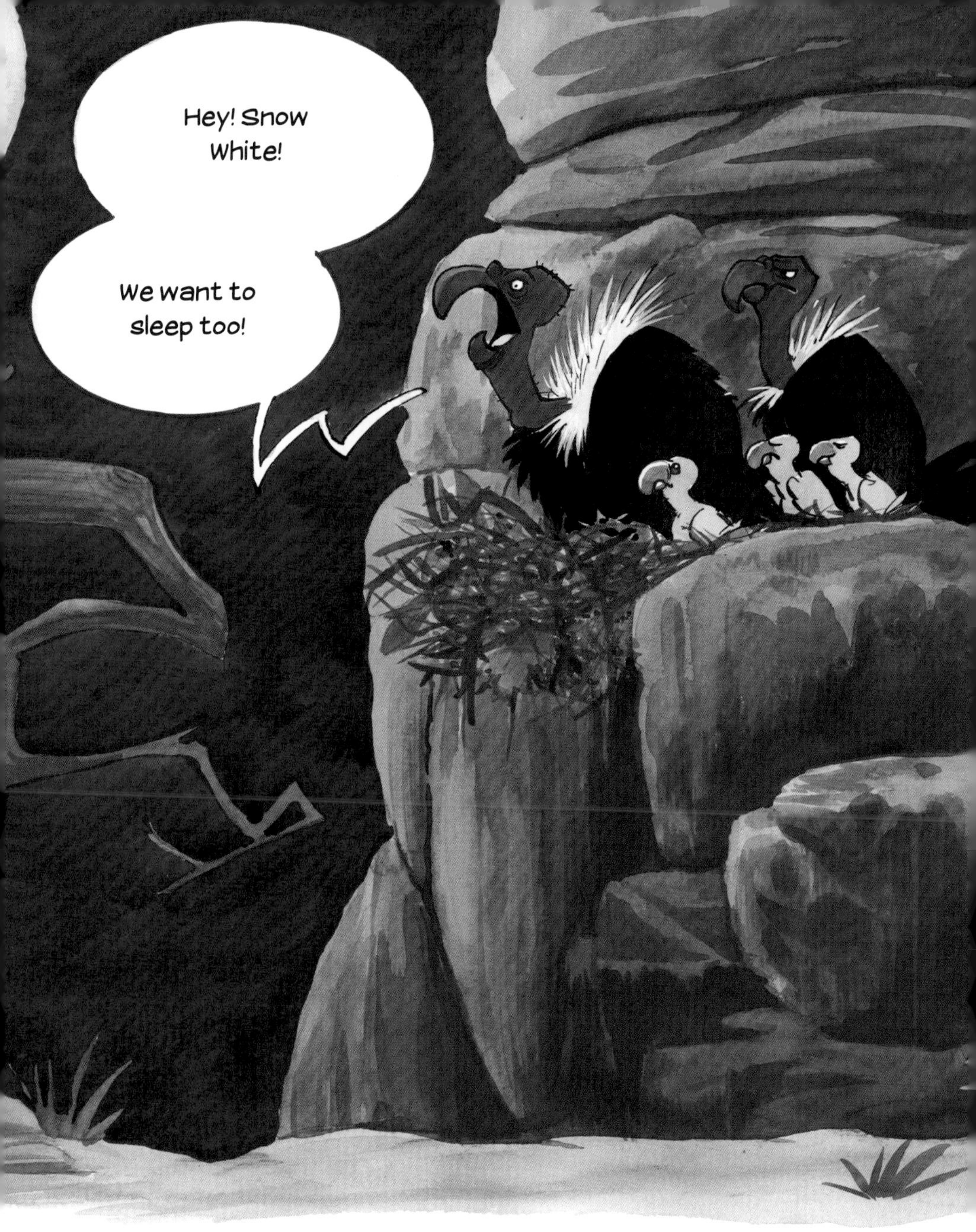
Hey! Snow White!
We want to sleep too!

If the lizard becomes too hot, its colours brighten up.

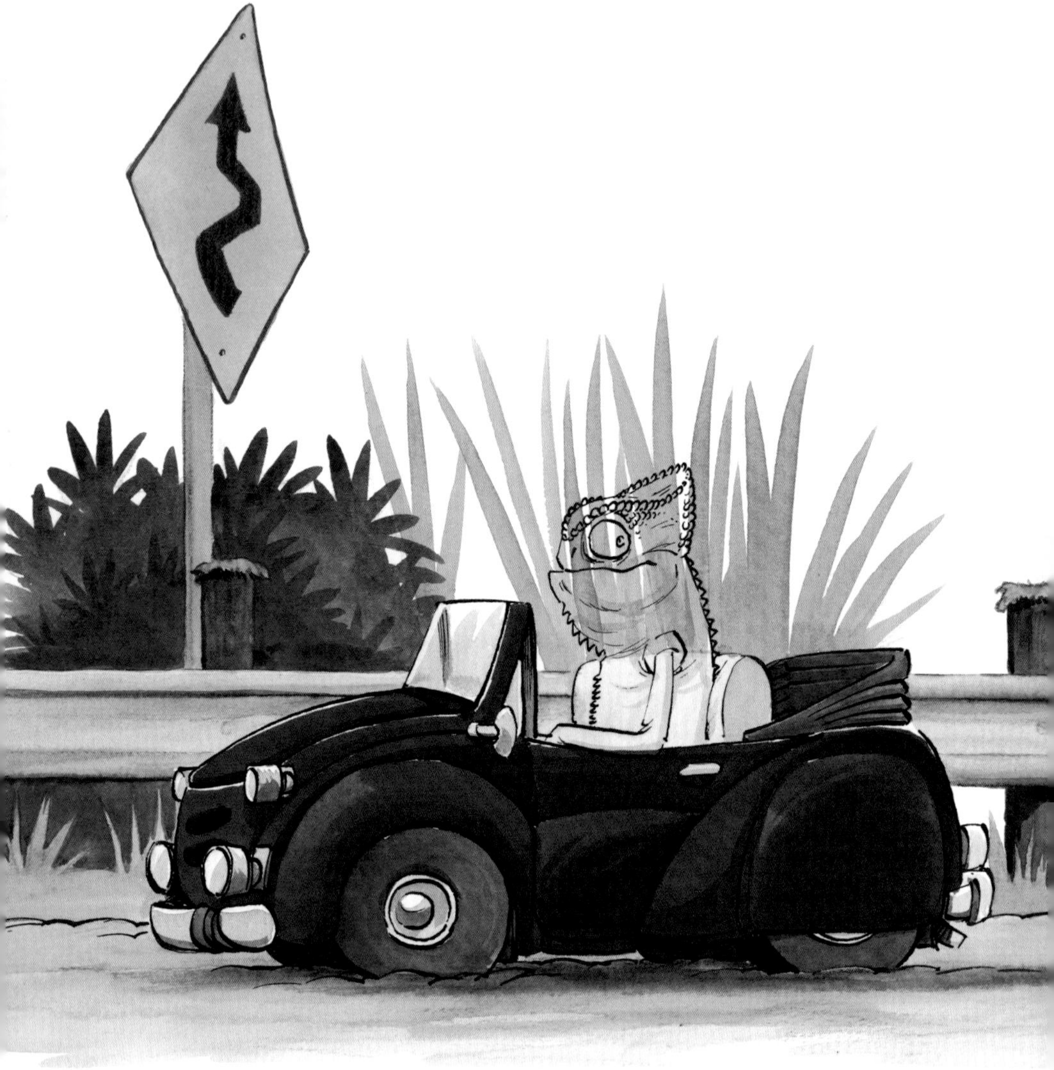

A chameleon's **camouflage** is its primary line of defence. If it feels threatened, it will stay motionless and try to blend into the surroundings by taking on a dull hue.

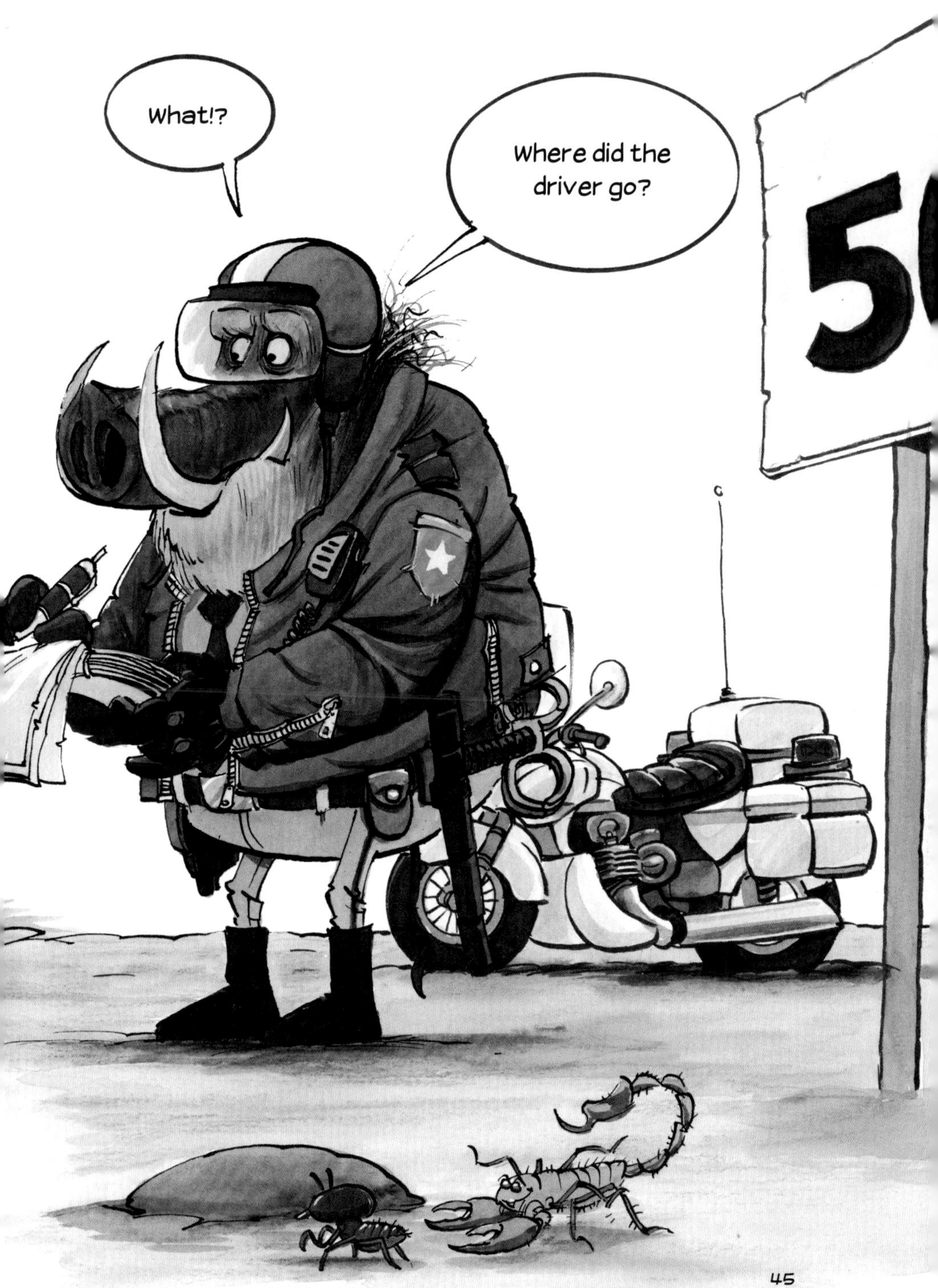

What!?
Where did the driver go?
50

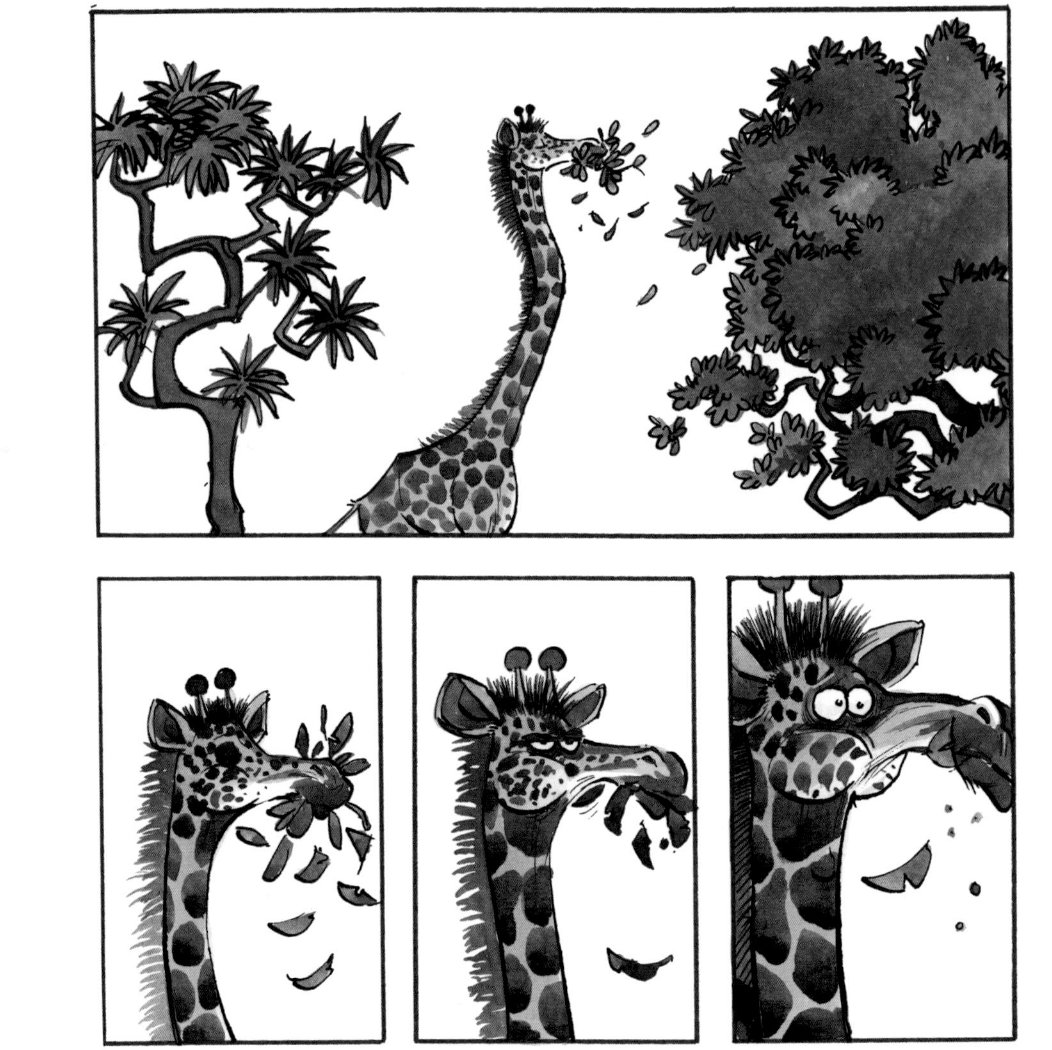

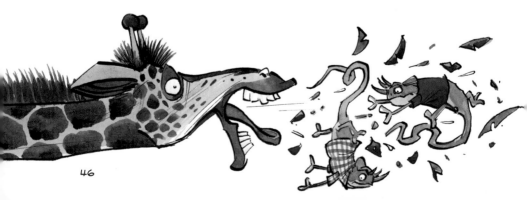

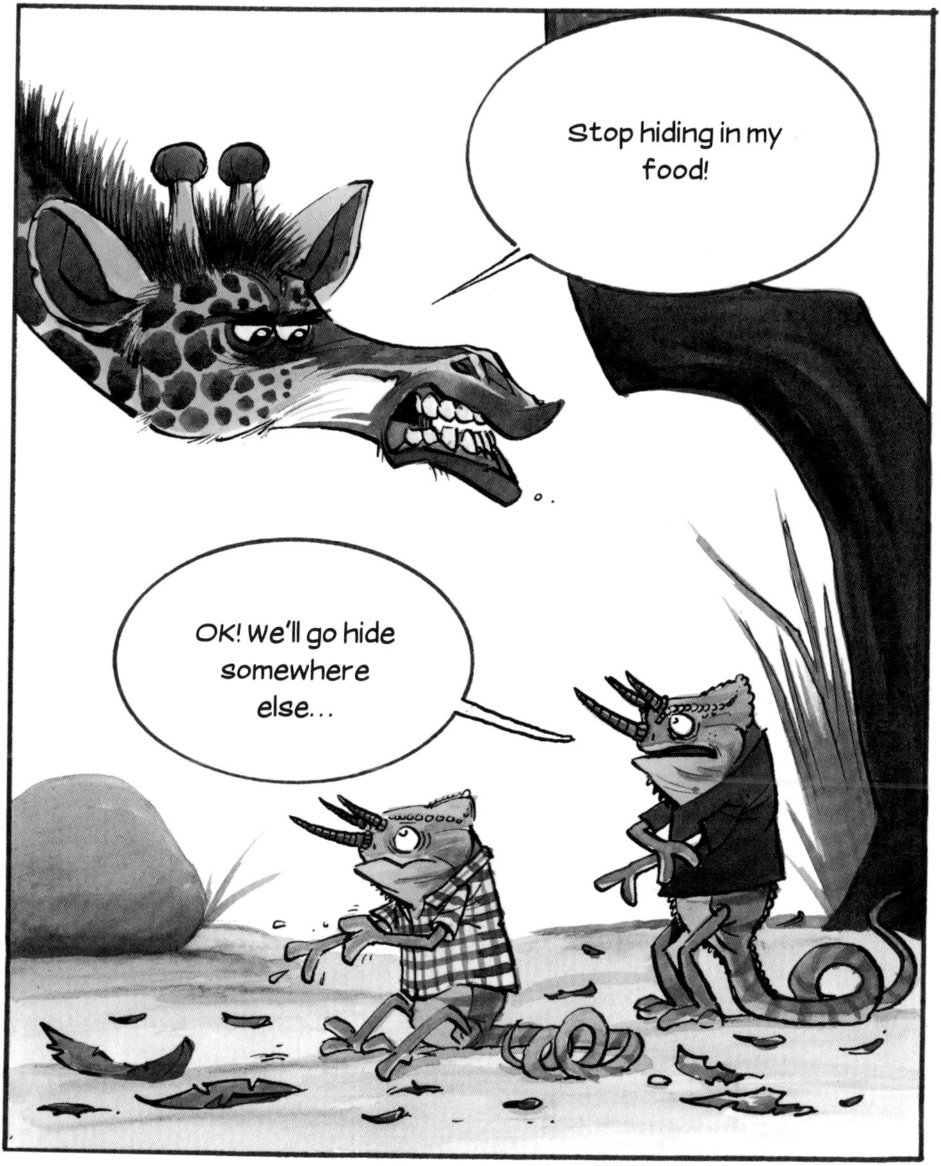
Stop hiding in my food!
OK! We'll go hide somewhere else...

The spikes, horns and other protuberances that adorn a chameleon's body help it blend into the foliage.

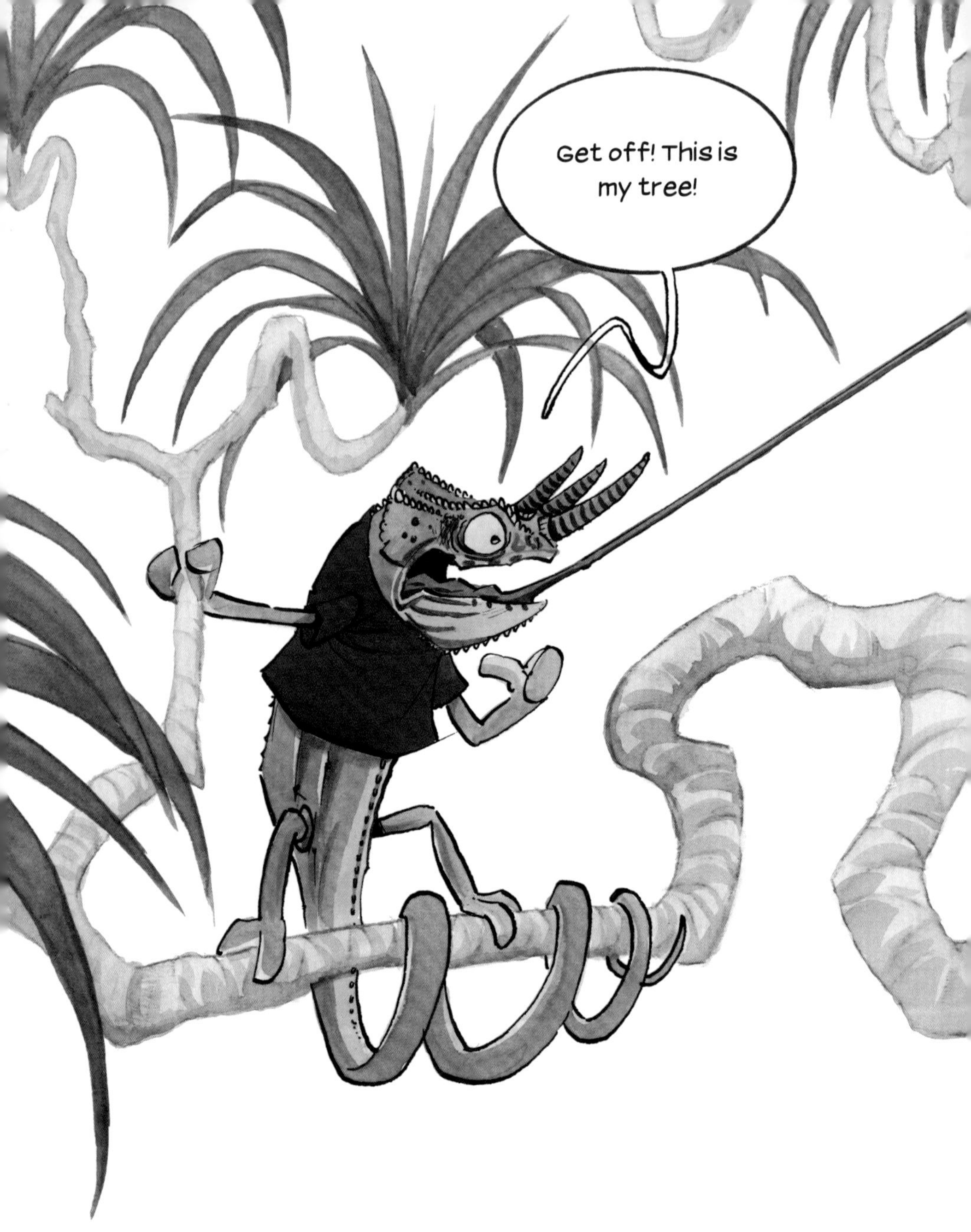
Get off! This is my tree!

This lizard lives a solitary life. It doesn't take kindly to any territorial intrusions, not even from its own species.

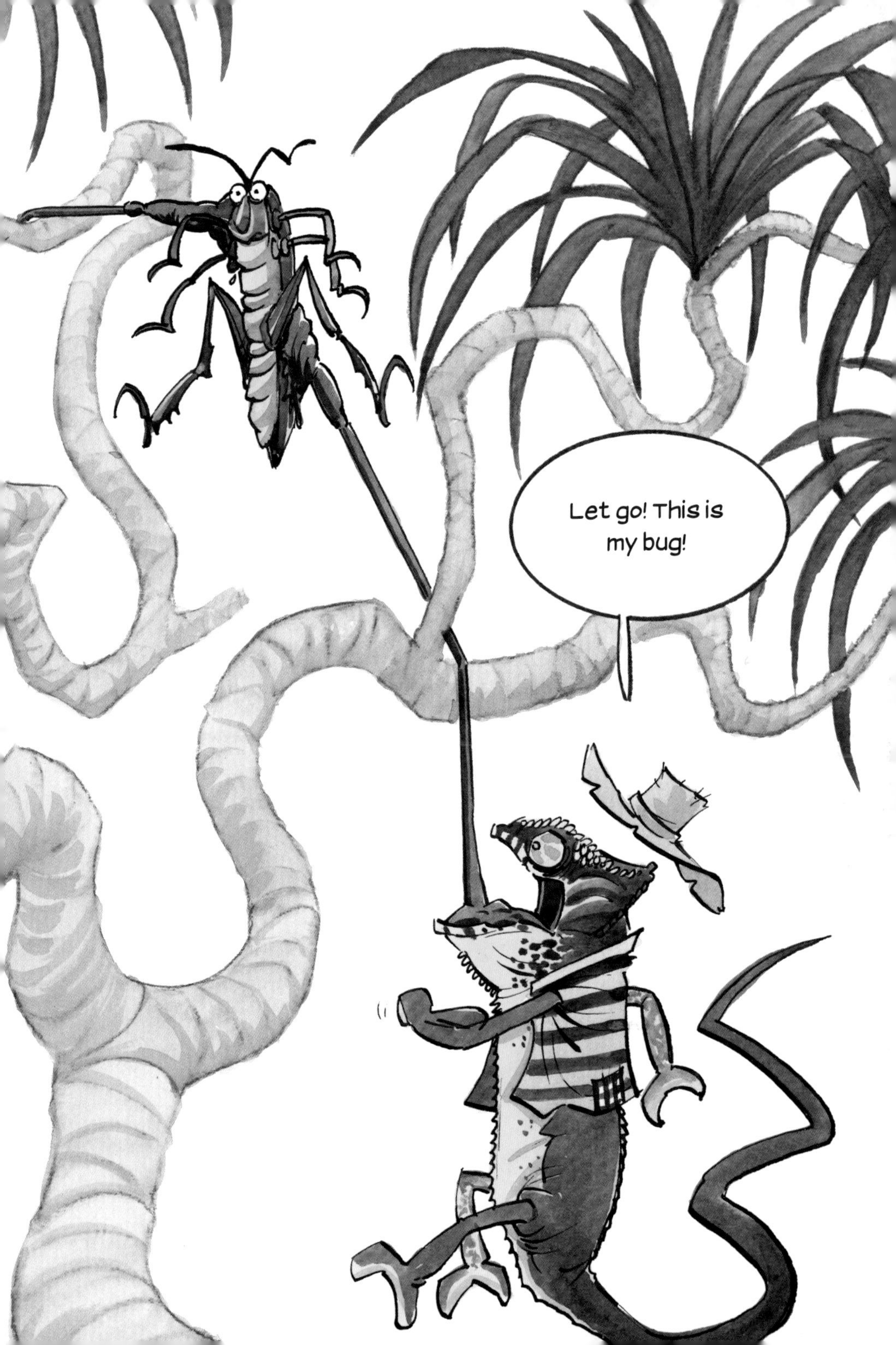
Let go! This is my bug!

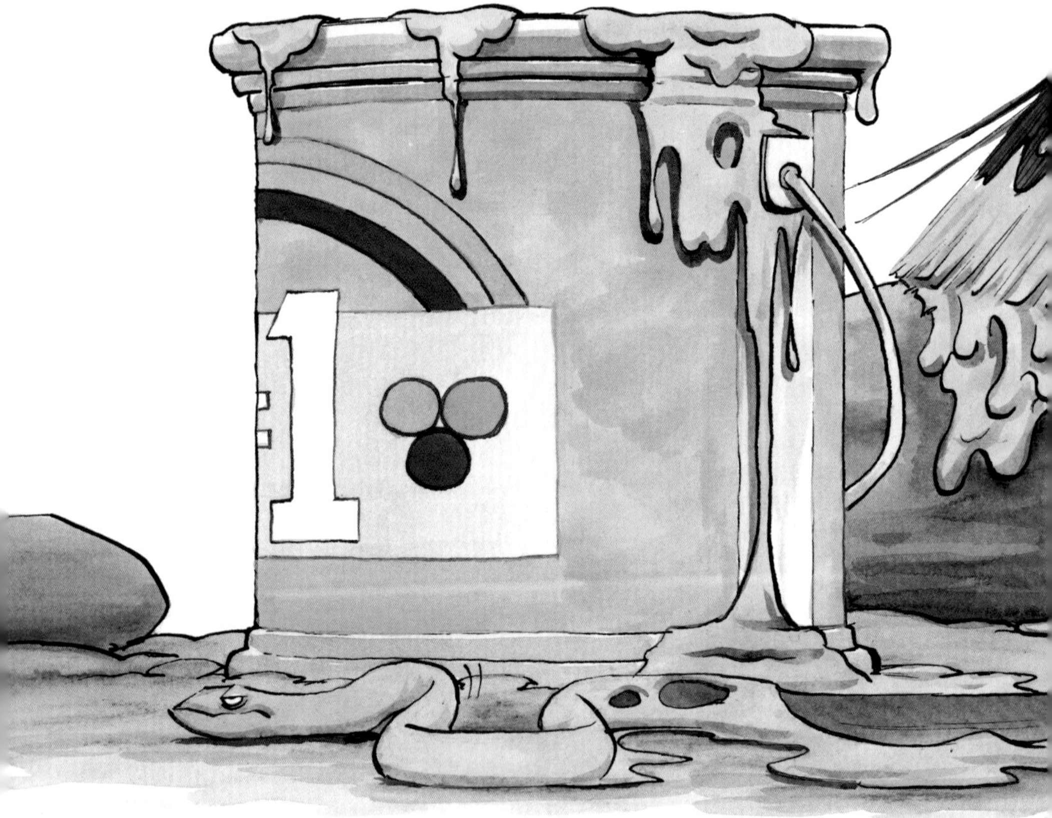
1

To be noticed during mating season, males become more colourful than usual. This way, they can impress females and intimidate rivals.

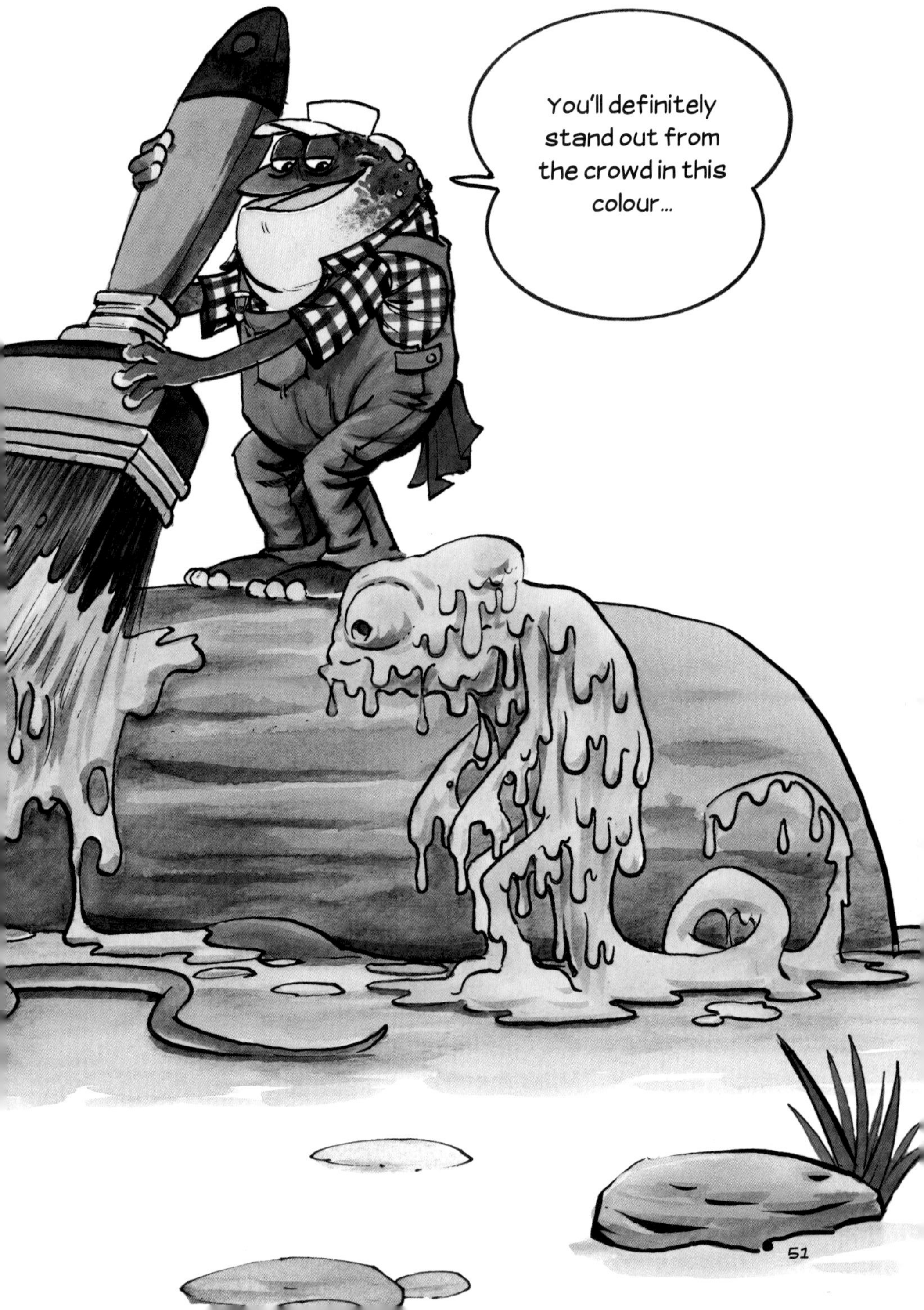
You'll definitely stand out from the crowd in this colour...

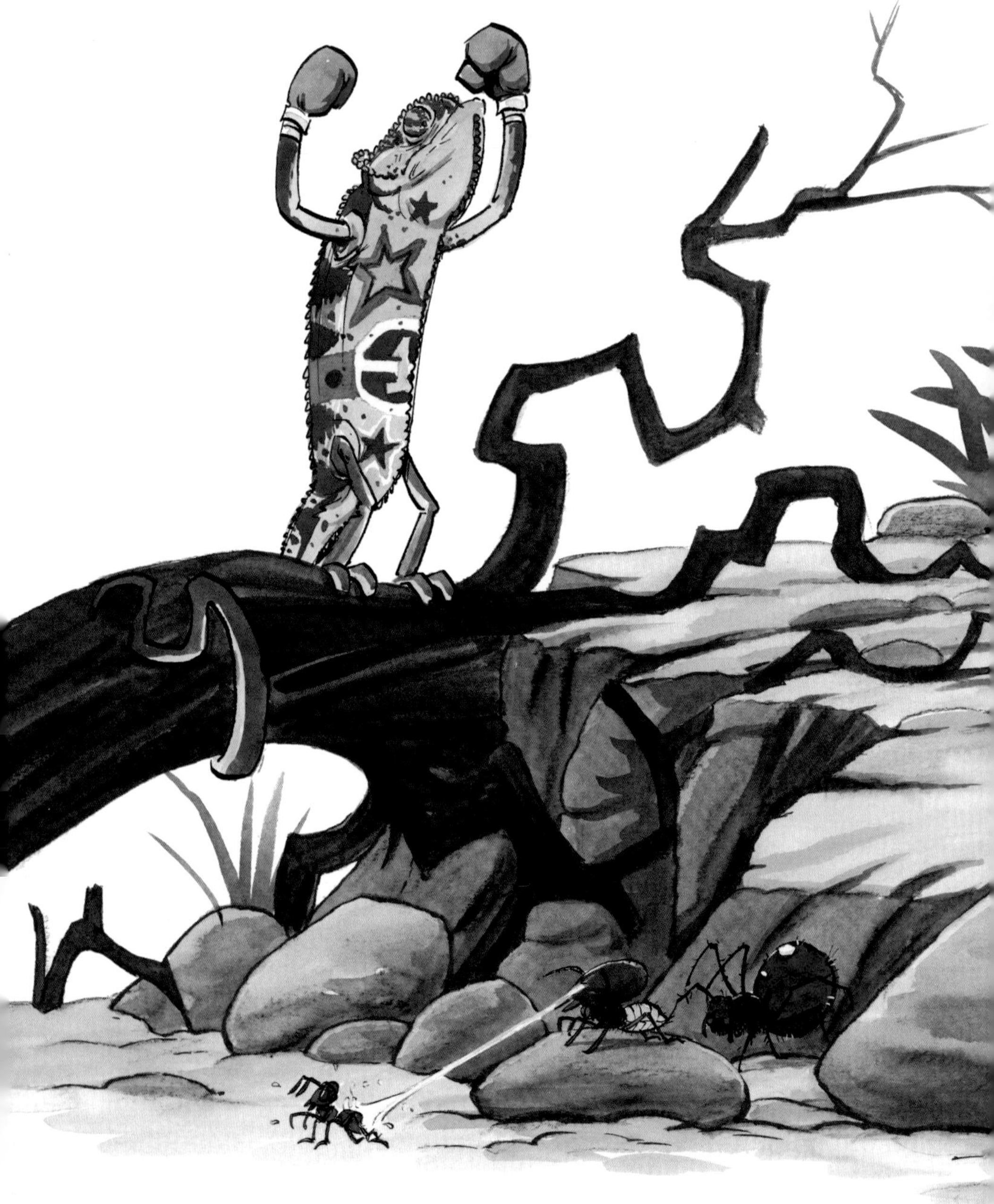

The winner of a chameleon fight will turn bright colours while the loser's colours will disappear as a sign of submission.

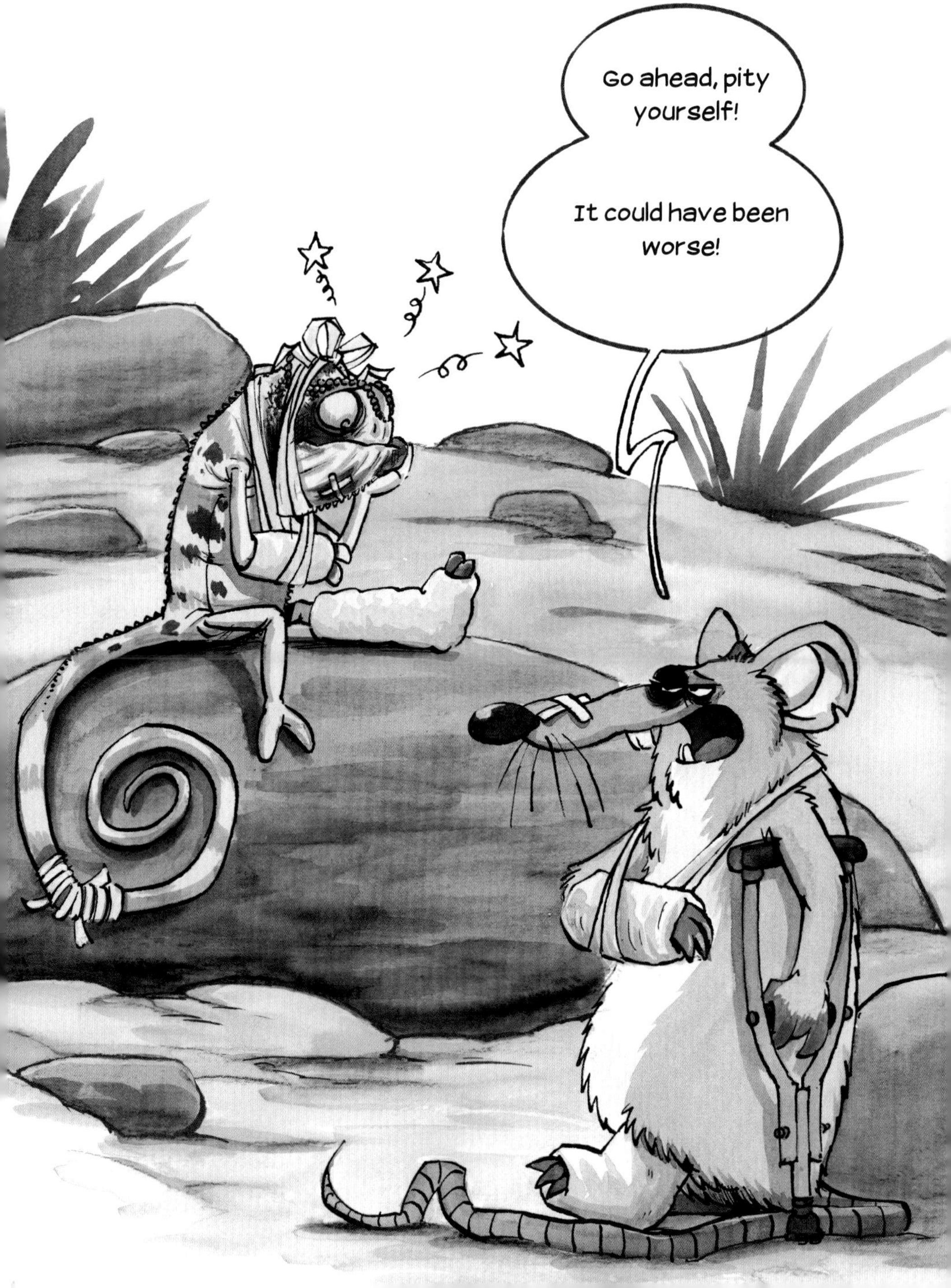
Go ahead, pity yourself!
It could have been worse!

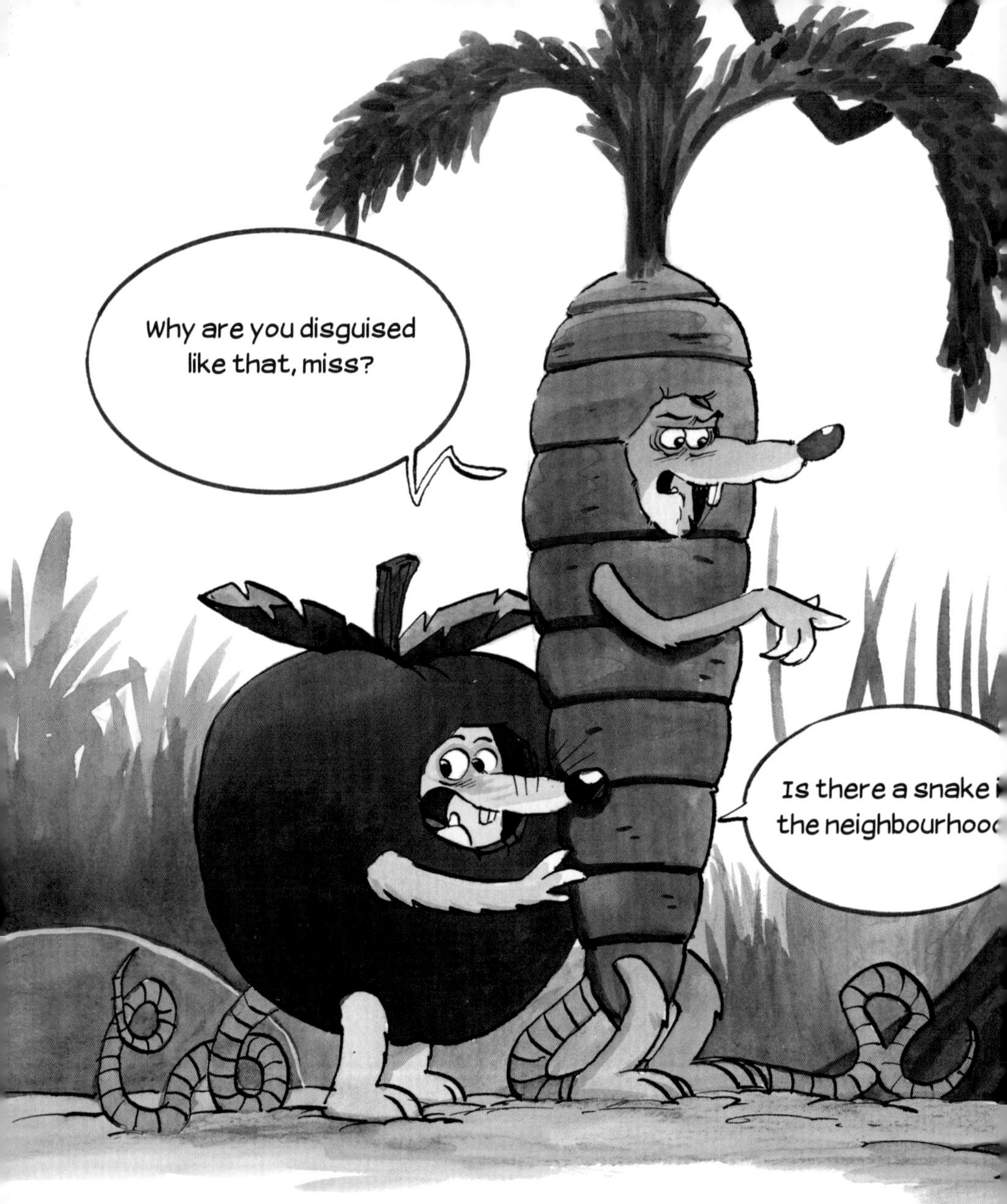
Why are you disguised like that, miss?
Is there a snake
the neighbourhoo

During a chameleon battle for a female mate, the female will wait passively for the outcome, camouflaged in surrounding foliage.

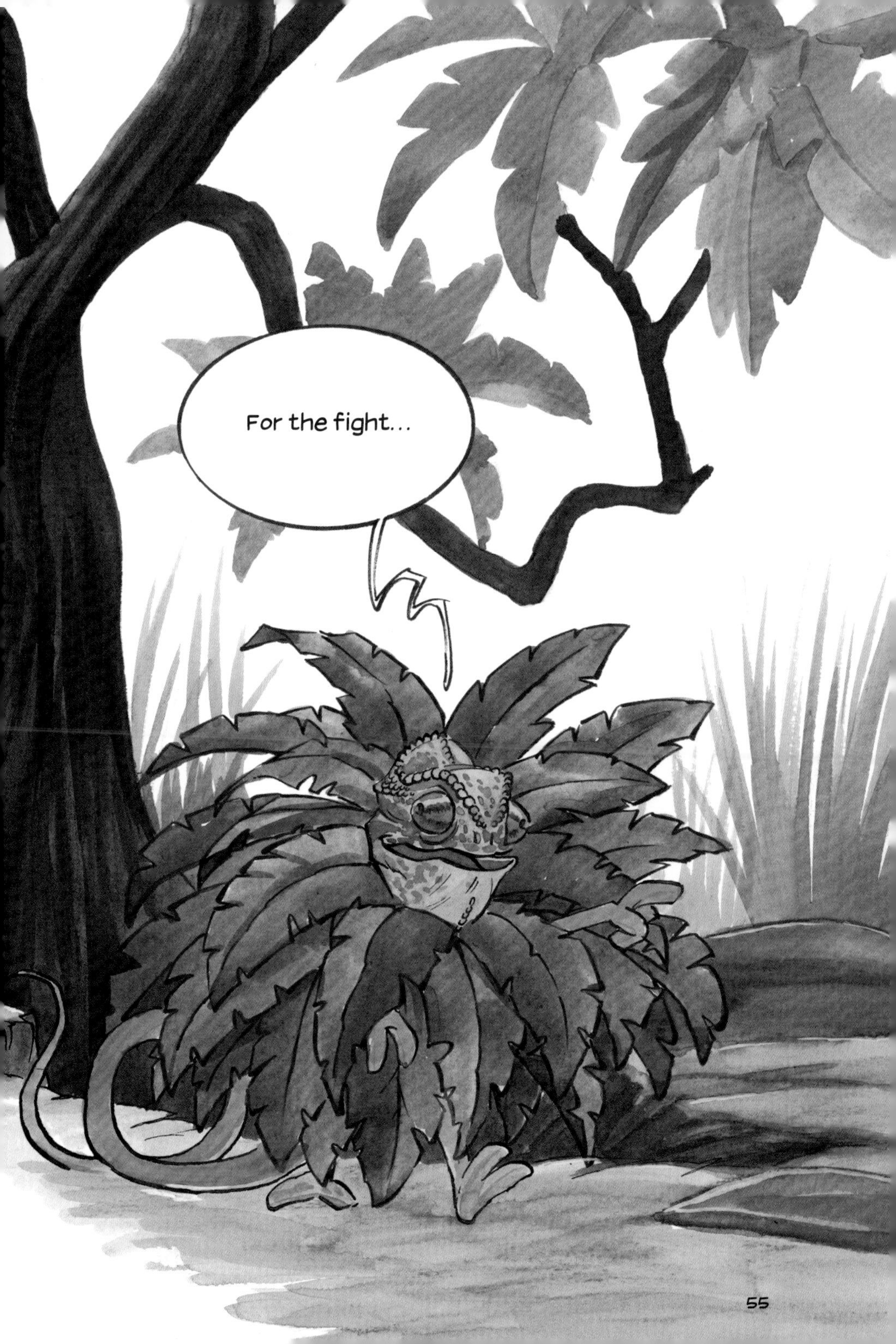
For the fight...

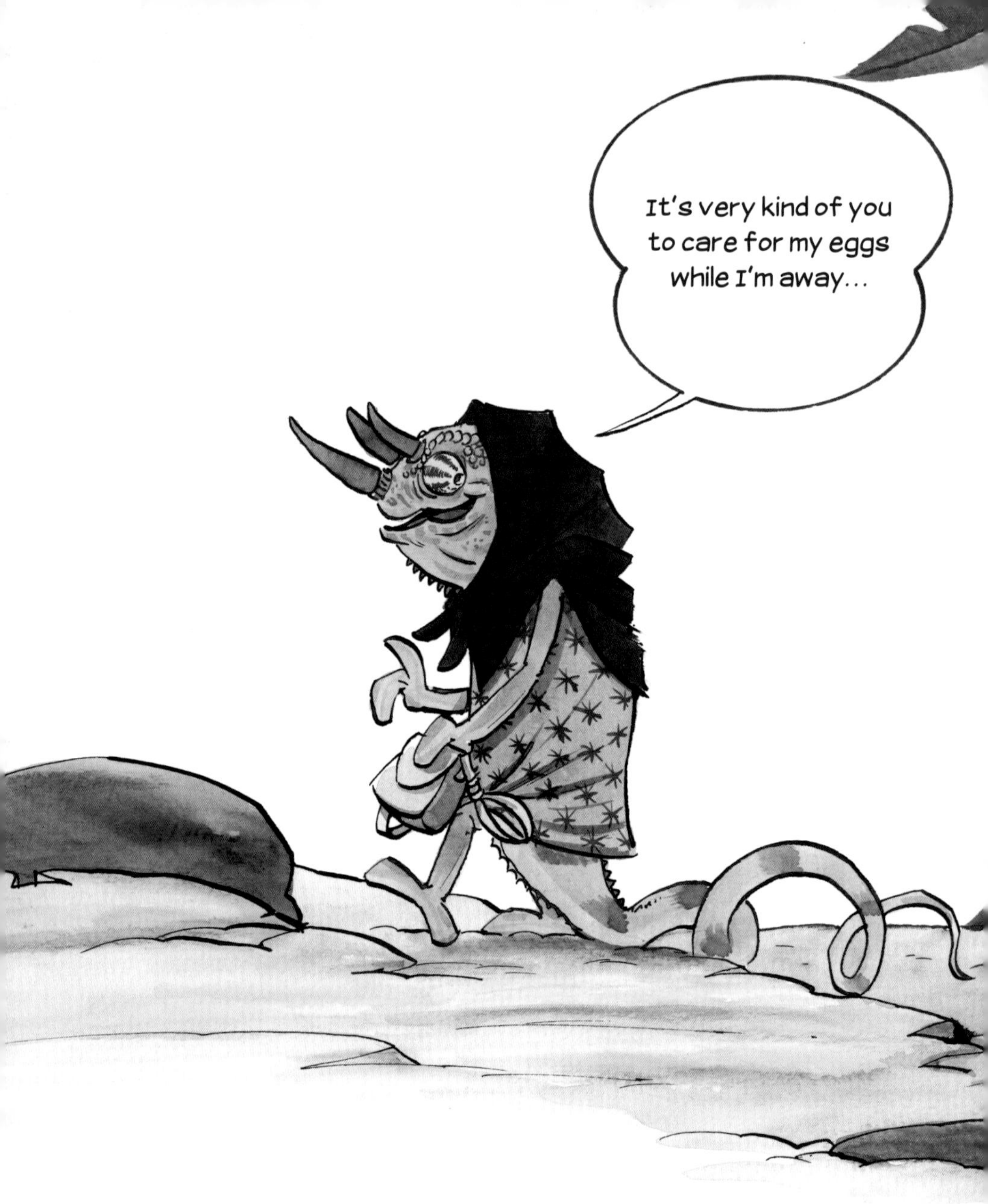
It's very kind of you to care for my eggs while I'm away...

While generally **oviparous**, a female chameleon lays from 4 to 40 eggs per brood. She abandons her eggs after depositing them into a nest that she has dug in the soil.

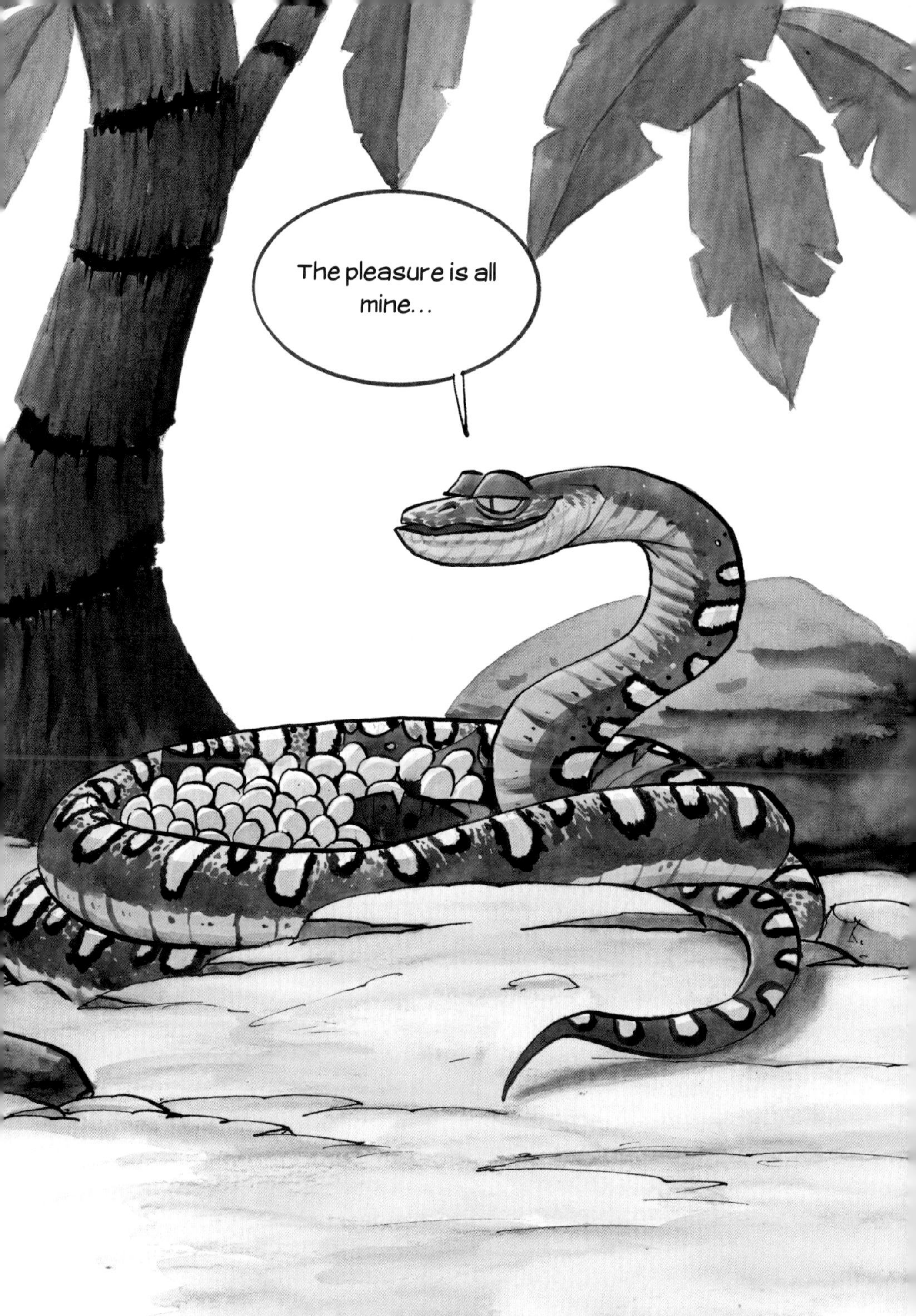
The pleasure is all mine...

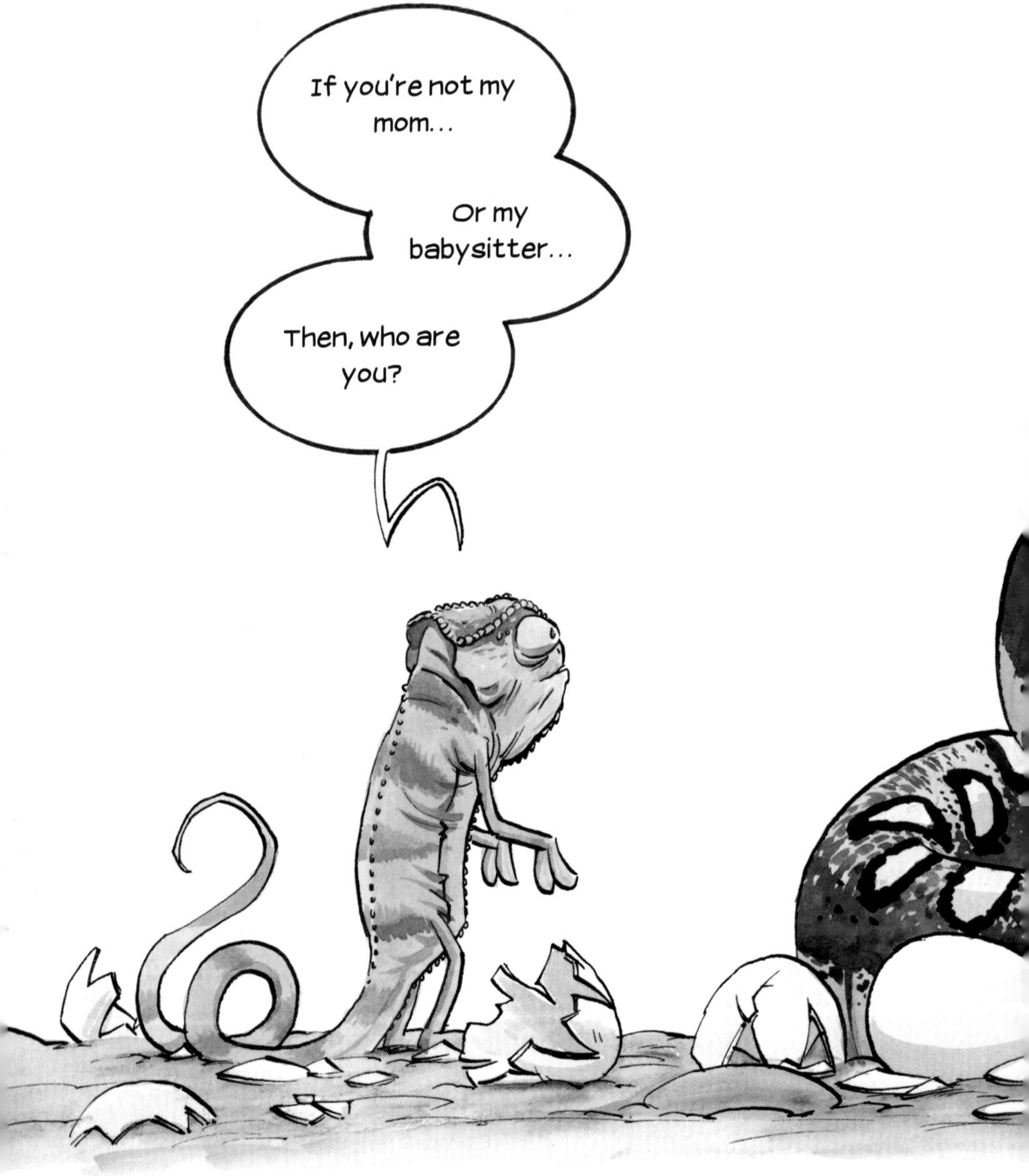
If you're not my mom...
Or my babysitter...
Then, who are you?

Once hatched from its egg, a young chameleon has to manage on its own. Just like an adult, it has to avoid enemies, daytime birds and arboreal snakes to survive.

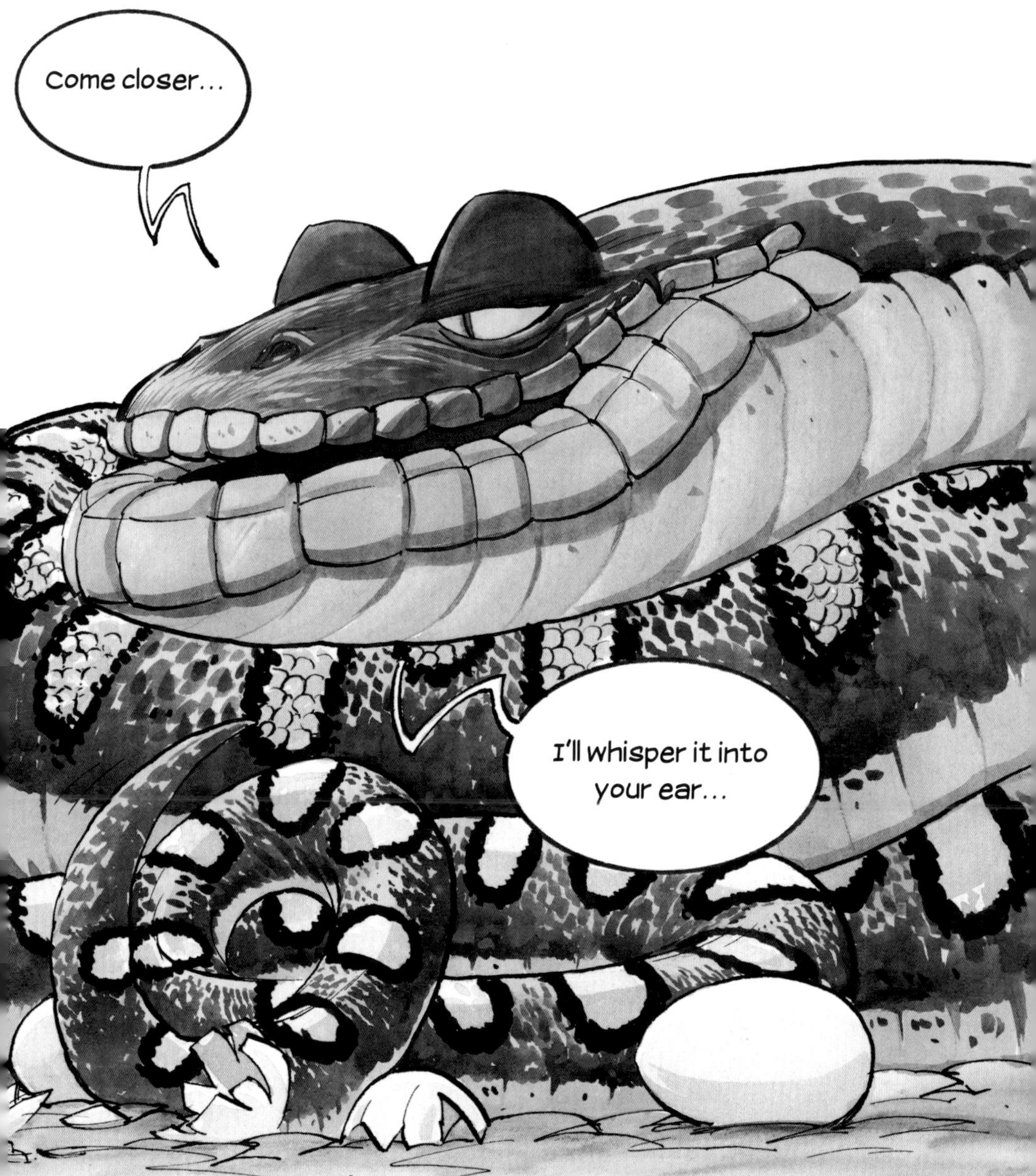
Come closer...
I'll whisper it into your ear...

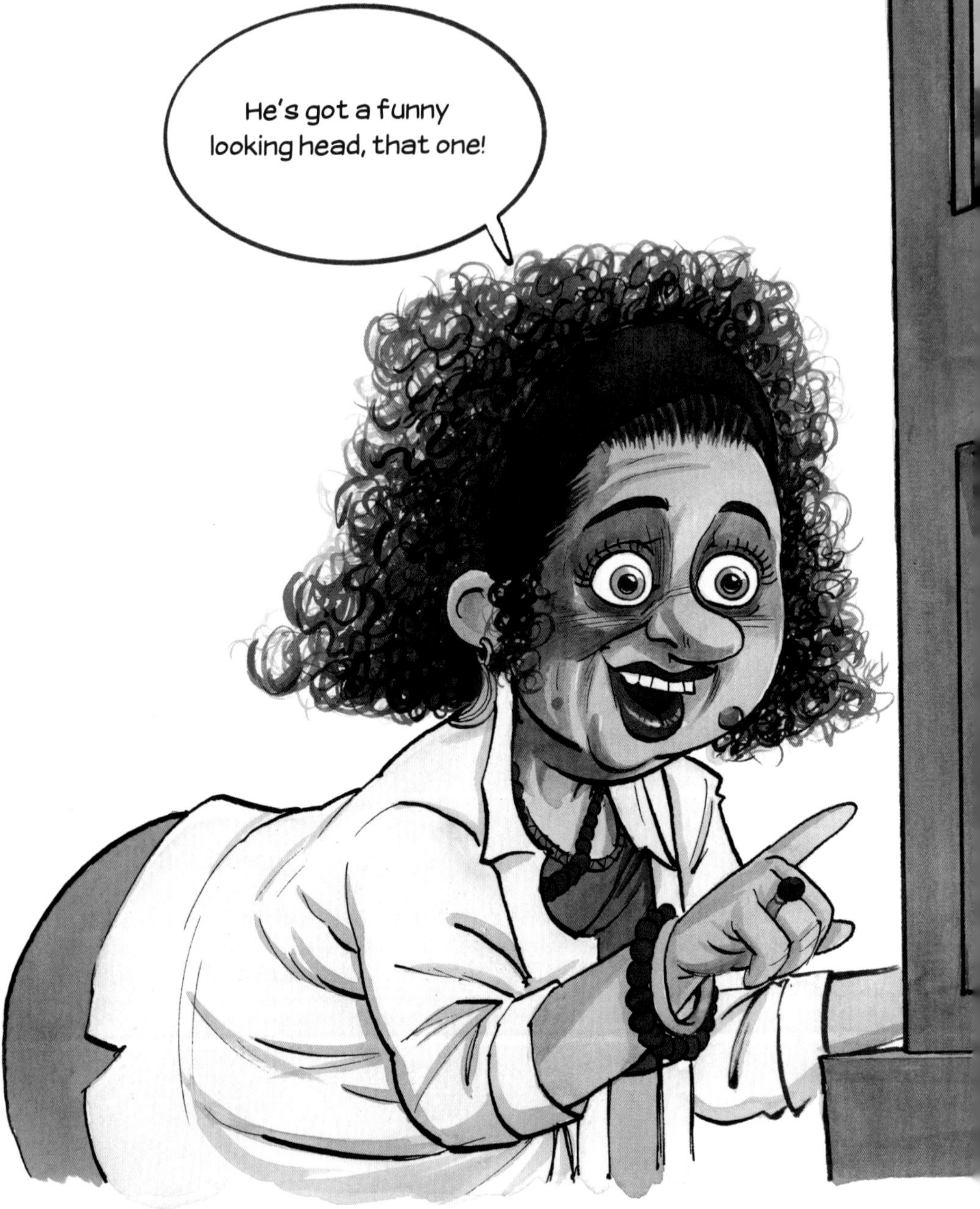
He's got a funny looking head, that one!

These harmless animals are threatened by humans. Among other things, people destroy chameleons' habitats, capture them to sell in pet shops and exterminate insects that they eat to survive.

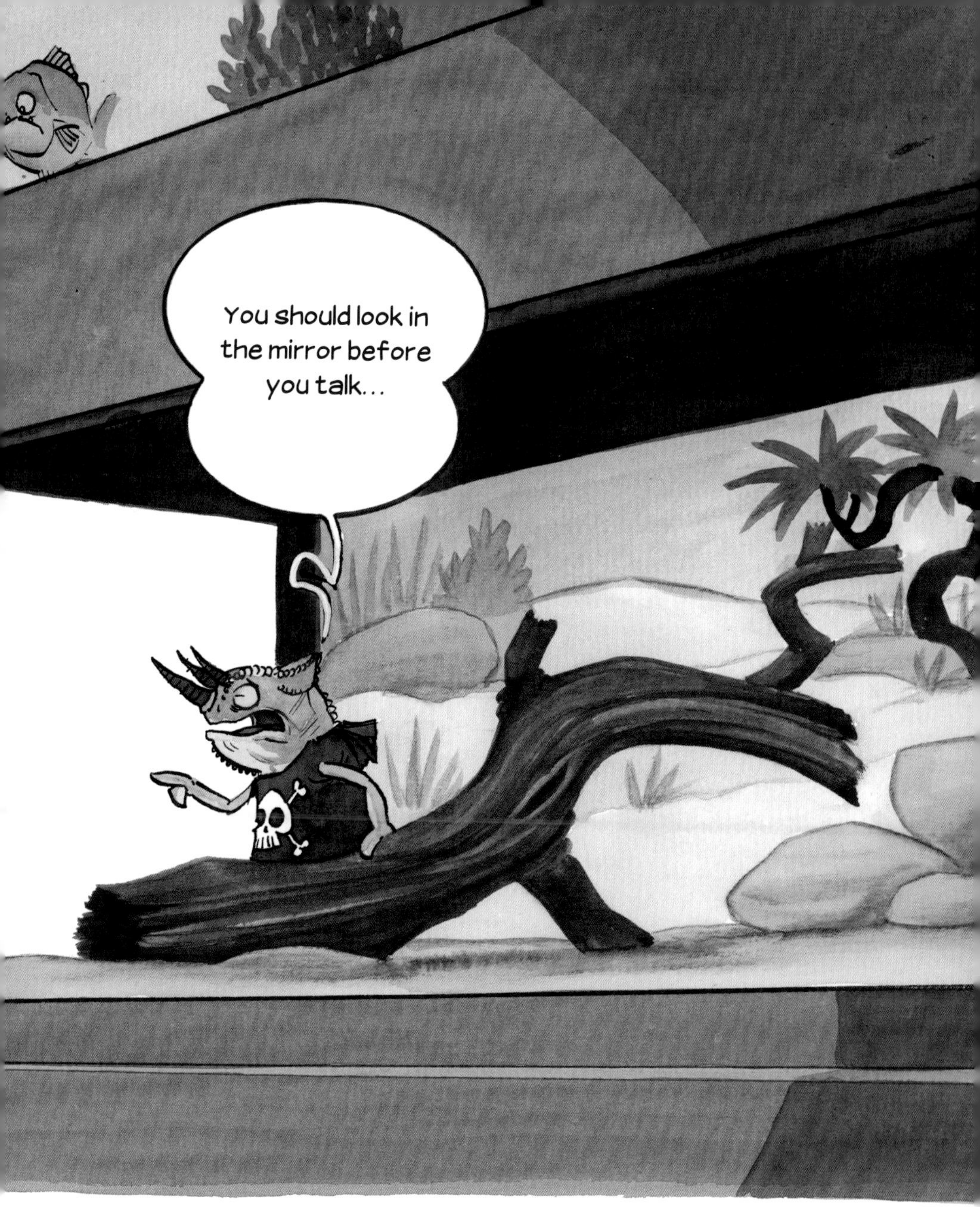
You should look in the mirror before you talk...

# Glossary

**Arboreal**  living in trees

**Camouflage**  blending into the environment to avoid detection

**Oviparous**  an animal that lays eggs

**Prehensile tail**  a tail that can grasp or hold onto objects

**Prey**  an organism hunted and killed by another for food

**Species**  a classification for a group of organisms with common characteristics

# Index

# Other *Do You Know?* titles

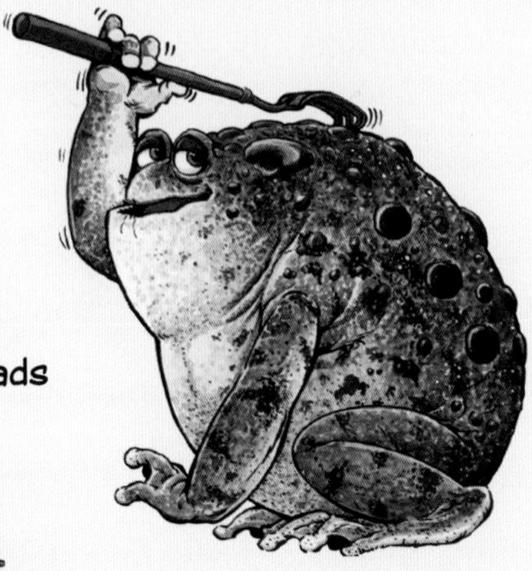

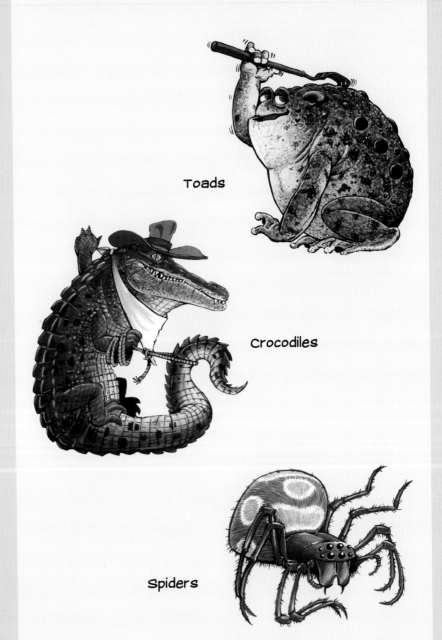

Toads

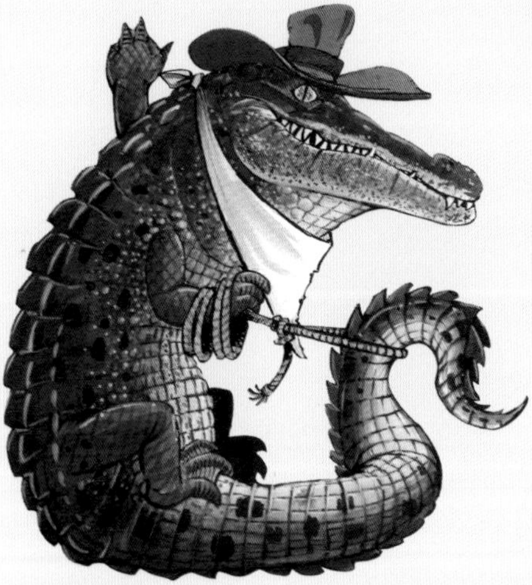

Crocodiles

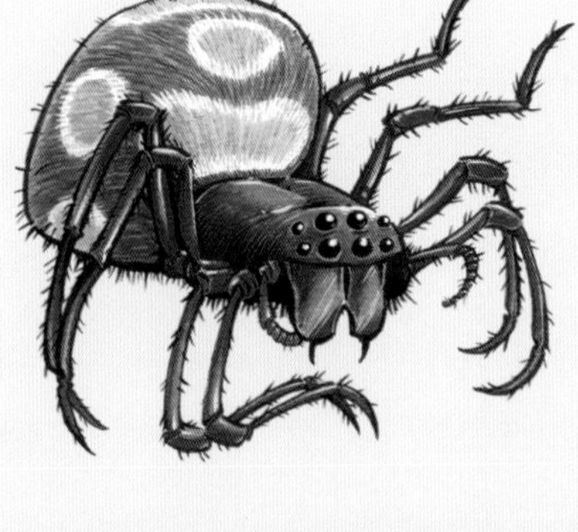

Spiders